Dont Let
hurt change
you
Donna

DYSFUNCTIONAL

. . .

ONE WOMAN'S STORY

D0615189

DEDICATION

This book is dedicated to my two sons, Dino and Nicholas, whom I love more than the air I breathe. Without them in my life, I don't know where I would be. Thank you for saving me.

Also, to a very special, young lady Joshy: I love you forever and ever. Keep making me proud.

And to my niece Skyla. Thank you for giving me a reason to go on in life; you are my sunshine. I love you with all my heart.

DISCLAIMER

The information and/or references in this book are of an inspirational nature only. The true names of each of the parties have been changed to protect each individual. The nature of this story is intended to show that life has many struggles, pains and disappointments and it takes courage and strength to work through them. No harm is intended to anyone connected with the story or reading its content. Although the author and the publisher have made every effort to ensure that the contents of this book were accurate at press time, the author and the publisher do not represent or devalue another person's perspective. The author and the publisher are not responsible for any disruption, loss or damage (including indirect or consequential damages) suffered by any party as a result of or in relation to the use of this book. To the extent permitted by law, the author and the publisher exclude any liability (including liability for negligence or

INTRODUCTION

As I sit in front of my computer and begin to put my book together, I am overwhelmed by the amount of emotion that flows through me. Although I started writing this over 30 years ago, I am finally ready to let the world read my story. Living through what happened is one thing but reliving each moment of what actually happened as an adult is draining. I have encountered many sleepless nights over this and a lot of physical pain just writing this. A young mind sees and understands things very differently than an adult mind. The purpose of writing this is to free myself from the pain which lies so deep inside of me. Also for everyone to know the truth... my truth.

I have spent the last three years worried about every aspect of this book. Until I came to the realization that there is no wrong or right way to write it out. This is my story and I am going to write it the way I remember it and share every emotional aspect of how I actually felt going through it. Many memories are short and others are longer (depending on my age and the impact at the time). My life has taken me through many storms and seasons but I made the decision to always stand up and face it head on. I hope that my story inspires at least one person to be strong and brave until the storm is over and on through the next. The strength we gain from each battle makes it easier to conquer the next obstacle every single time. It is possible to grow a little more each day. You are always stronger than you believe yourself to be.

Greenpoint, Brooklyn is the neighborhood I lived in. On a lovely tree lined street, directly across from a beautiful park and surrounded by many friendly neighbors and families similar to mine. Or at least that's what I thought. Then there was my house. It was the only red house on the block and I thought it was special.

I am about four years old when this story begins. I remember being tall for my age. I had light blonde hair, green eyes, pink cheeks, and rosy red lips. I lived with my mother who was a short, stocky woman with blonde hair and blue eyes. She wore her hair in a beehive sixties hairstyle (which was the trend of her time even though it was already the early seventies). She was a master at it. It was always perfect. As astonishing as her hairstyle was, I found it weird that she didn't have any teeth. I would find out why later in life. My brother Peter was tall like me but he had brown hair and brown eyes. However, my other brother, Paul, looked more like my mom (with the blond hair and blue eyes).

My parents separated when I was two and my father went to live in Bensonhurst, Brooklyn with his mother. He was tall with dark features; kind of looked like Elvis. He always seemed to make me happy.

Now being a young girl, I would listen to stories my mom told me about her life. She always spoke about her grandmother who was a great mom to all of her children. She spoke about how good she was to her and how they baked cookies together. For a while, I thought my mother had a great childhood because her stories always made me feel all warm inside. That is of course until she began to tell me about her own mother. My mother said she never got along with her mom and insisted her mom did not love her. When my mother was six years old, my grandmother sent her to live in an orphanage that was run by nuns in upstate New York. When I asked her why my grandmother sent her away or why she didn't love her: my mother would always say her mom called her an unruly child. I never knew what that meant. Another reason she would give me is that her mom got divorced and met a new man who didn't want children.

At that time, I couldn't understand it. I couldn't understand why she couldn't live with her own grandmother, whom she adored. I guess back then they did what they thought was best for my mom. I will never know the real truth behind it. It just didn't make sense to me. Even when my mother was a teenager and came out of the orphanage, her mother still seemed to be estranged from her. We hardly ever saw our grandmother.

In my house it was mom, my two brothers and I. From what I remember we were always running around, playing and stuff. I remember Peter would take us to the park in the early hours of the morning (even before our mom got up). This was something we did often. I thought it was normal at the time because I was young and didn't know any better. Most of the time, my brothers and I didn't even have clothes on. Sometimes

Peter would even forget us there because he was so busy playing. Life just seemed fun and carefree at time.

Then my great grandfather came to live with us. He wasn't a very nice man. He seemed to hate the world (and strongly disliked children). I didn't know why he was there but he was scary. He would walk around the house cursing at us for no reason. He would call us things like "cocksuckers", "grease balls", and "no good little bastards". I never knew why he didn't like us or why my mother allowed him to talk that way to us. I remember that he would also pee out the window on all the kids playing downstairs and the neighbors would complain to my mother all the time. One day, she actually nailed his window shut so that he couldn't do it again.

He lived with us for about a year. I came home one day and he wasn't there. I asked where Poppa was and my mom replied that "the old bastard died". I don't remember feeling sad over his death. In fact, I was kind of happy because he was scary to all of us. I remember my mom telling people that her grandfather died... as if she actually cared for him. She was never nice to him but somehow enjoyed it when people told her that they were "sorry about her loss". I thought that her behavior was strange. I was young. Just a kid. I didn't understand. Now as an adult, I have a better understanding of where it all began. At this point, I began to study her behavior because I was really confused and knew something wasn't right.

However, my grandmother didn't seem to care about her father dying. Everybody went on with their lives as though nothing had happened. My grandmother owned a restaurant right up the block from us. She never seemed to come over to visit us. As a child, I would walk up the block sometimes naked with a penny to buy bubblegum from the gumball machine that she had at her restaurant. When I got there, she would send me back home the same way I showed up, without clothes on and all alone. She never once tried to bring me home herself.

I guess she figured that if I got there alone, I could just as well return home alone. I can only imagine how long I was doing this while being completely oblivious to what was really going on around me. I now have a clearer understanding of what was wrong with how these adults were taking care and responsibility over me. But at the time, I was just slightly aware that they didn't even realize I had left the house.

I do recall that when I played outside with my brothers, my mother would never be out there with us. I used to see the other moms and dads with their kids. I don't have any memories of her taking us to the park. Or anywhere for that matter. I don't have much memory of that Greenpoint apartment but I do remember my mom always had the ironing board open to iron the curtains.

One day, I ran upstairs and grabbed the cup my mother had on the ironing board and drank it really fast. Out of nowhere, she came in and dragged me to the kitchen while sticking her fingers down my throat. I threw up everything I drank (which by the way tasted like shit). After all the picking me up, dragging me to the sink, making me throw up, and scaring me so bad, my mother never told me why she did that. I remember crying so much from how horrible it all felt. I later found out from my brother that it was her scotch. That memory is etched in my brain and it caused me to be scared to drink anything she offered me after that.

~*
~

When I came home one day, there was a boy in my house. I asked my mother about him. She informed me that it was my brother and his name was Bob. I asked where he came from and she simply told me that I had other siblings who did not live with us. She wouldn't tell me anything else but to go play. I remember staring at Bob. He wasn't happy. He seemed so sad and alone, sitting in the corner of the room . He didn't speak much and kept to himself. He was about fifteen years old at the time.

As soon as Bob got there, my mother made him take us everywhere whether he wanted to or not. It wasn't until a summer day out in the park with Bob that I decided to ask him where he lived before he came to live with us. He told me he lived with his other mother and wanted to go back there. I asked him why he doesn't just go back. That's when he told me that they didn't want him anymore. The sadness in his eyes always made him look like he wanted to cry. I just grabbed his hand and started walking with him. I realized then that he was here to stay.

On Sundays, my father would pick us up and take us out for the day. He never took Bob with us when we went out. I never understood why but my mother would always yell at my dad saying, "You only give me ten dollars a week for three kids." That was her famous quote. He would never respond. My father was very nice to me and gave us lots of hugs and kisses which was something my mother never gave us. He always made me feel special. We would go to Coney Island, to the beach, or to his house to spend time with our grandmother who was also very nice to me. We would also go to my aunt's house so we could spend time with our cousins. Spending time with my father at this age was always very pleasant for me. He treated me and my brothers very well but I would soon learn that at that age we don't always understand everything.

We had many friends and neighbors on the block but one woman in particular was close to my mom. Her name was Samantha and she had seven children. She lost her husband to lung cancer two years prior to meeting my mother. Samantha was pregnant with her eighth child. It seemed that my mother was trying to help her and she seemed to help my mother. At the time, she had all of her children living with her. One of her daughters, Annmarie (who was about sixteen at the time) was a great help to her.

Annmarie was tending to her siblings, cooking meals, and cleaning the house. She would take us all to the park multiple times a week. We would go to Samantha's house all the time. She was a happy woman and was always laughing. Samantha would ask my brothers to rub her legs all the time. She had very large veins on her legs that would hurt her. My brothers would take turns rubbing her legs for hours which made her very happy.

Annmarie would also be at our house every day. It was great when she was there because she would always take care of us and make us food. This is around the time I began to notice my mother manipulating Annmarie. My mother would drink with her. She would constantly ask Annmarie for money. It always confused me why my mother would get so angry when Annmarie wanted to go home.

I was playing with my dolls and Annmarie when out of nowhere she begins to have pains in her stomach. She goes to the hospital with my mother. When my mother comes back she tells us that Annmarie had a baby and she named her Bippy. She was very small. Bippy was four pounds and seven ounces and only seventeen and a half inches long. After a couple of days, my mother comes home with Annmarie and the baby. I remember when I first saw the baby, I thought about how small she was. She looked like a doll. My mother tended to the baby and seemed to care about her. I had never seen my mother show affection until this point.

After Bippy's birth, Annmarie decided to move in with us. Her family was in constant contact with her in order to make sure she was okay. Yet they always asked her to go back home (as well as insisted she not drink anymore). Although Annmarie would always promise not to, it was just a lie. Life seemed to be changing once the baby arrived. Yet all that I could think about was Bippy. I would play with her as though she was my doll. Samantha gave birth to her last child and no longer spoke to my mother.

One day, I came home to find everything in the house packed in boxes. My mother told us we were moving. I remember that I cried and I asked her where we were going. She said that we were going back to where we used to live: Bensonhurst, Brooklyn. I started to cry because I didn't want to leave my friends. After about an hour there was a truck outside. My brothers and Annmarie carried our stuff to the truck. Just like that, we didn't live there anymore. I didn't even get to say goodbye to my friends or my neighbors. No one.

Living in Bensonhurst, I remember that apartment vividly. It was a big apartment with lots of rooms. I remember that there was a lot of space compared to the other apartment. While living there, my brothers and I would go to the Cadets every day. I remember wearing uniforms and Bob holding the flag. It was like the army. We would line up, march, and say commands. It was fun for me. At this time, I remember my mother drinking alcohol, playing music loudly, and dancing around the house. This was the beginning of what became the norm.

On a Monday night, I came home from the Cadets and my grandmother was there. This was very odd since she never came to visit us. My grandmother had two teenagers with her. I asked her, "Nanny, who is that?" and she told me, "That's your sister." Once again, I'm standing there confused. So I asked my mother, "Who is it?" and she said, "It's your sister, Betty." Then she begins to tell me that she was married to Betty's father and came home one day to find him cheating on her with the babysitter. She walked out on him, leaving the children behind. She had three children with him whose names were Bob, Betty and Cora. After my mother left him, he didn't want the children either. Bob and Betty went to go live with two of my mother's aunts and Cora went to go live with her father's brother. Neither one of them raised the three children.

While my sister was visiting with her husband, it seemed like there wasn't any connection between her and my mother at all. Betty seemed very nice and quiet but after the younger children went to bed there was a lot of yelling going on between my mother, Betty, and my grandmother. There was a lot of talk about who didn't do what and who didn't take care of whom. I didn't understand all of it but I sat there for days wondering how my mother left her children and never talked about them. It's as though they never existed. This didn't make any sense to me. I might have been young and perhaps I didn't know much about life but I knew this was wrong.

My sister stayed for a few days. While she was there, Betty and her husband made a sandwich out of cat food and fed it to my grandmother. They laughed about it even with my mother. Even though my grandmother didn't like me, I thought that was very mean. They drank, they argued and she left. I never saw her again. I began to wonder how long it would take my mom to get rid of us. This was a burden I carried for a long time.

~*~

I never remembered my mother showing me love as I grew up. I soon came to the realization that the love was never there. At a very young age, I began to listen closely to what she was saying and who she was saying it to. I learned to differentiate between truth and lies. This is when I realized that my mother was drinking alcohol every day, she had no money, and she was unemployed. There was never any food in the refrigerator. She always relied on Annmarie to get her money. The landlord would constantly knock on the door for rent. I learned what it was to be hungry and soon realized this feeling wasn't new. I loved my mother and I never wanted to ask her for anything. It seemed like every time we asked her for something, she would yell at us as if we were bothering her. As if we were a burden. Even if it was just for food.

Six months later, I come home from school and again, I find the entire apartment filled with boxes and mom telling us we're moving. Now, this time I knew why we were moving. She didn't pay the rent. Once again, there were no goodbyes to friends, teachers... no one. We put our stuff in the truck and we were back on our way to Greenpoint, Brooklyn. My mother rented an apartment on Nassau Avenue. This apartment was small. I remember it had a bathtub in the kitchen and one in the bathroom. I wondered how we would take a bath in the kitchen. It was my mother, my three brothers and I living there. The real chaos began in this apartment. There were many people drinking, smoking cigarettes, and coming in and out of the house. I would often wake up to different people sleeping over.

At this point, I noticed my mother had a friend, a woman named Jean, who I thought was a man at first. Jean was always at the apartment with my mother. They were always drinking and smoking; at this time my mother started going out. She was at the bar all the time. Jean and my mother would always get into fights: punching, slapping, and cursing... the works. Us kids were sent to the back room while all this went on. I wanted to see what was going on in the kitchen. I wasn't that little kid anymore. I was curious. I saw my mother kissing Jean and at that time I didn't know that two women could kiss. From what I saw, I believed it to be something bad because of all the violence between them.

My brother Bob was miserable at this point. I guess he understood more of what was going on than I did. My mother would constantly pick on him. Bob didn't like to take baths. One day she had company over and I remember her sending us to the back room. I could hear Bob crying. She made him stand in the bathtub in the middle of the kitchen in front of all of her friends and began to scrub his body with one of those wire brushes used to scrub floors. Bob screams horrified me as I watched him from the back room. He was trying to cover his private parts which were red and swollen. I'm not sure if it was from him being dirty or if my mother had already gotten him with the wire brush. She did that to embarrass him. She could have used the bathtub in the bathroom but chose not to. From that moment on I became terrified of my mother.

Her idea of bathing Peter, Paul and me was to fill the bathtub in the bathroom and tell us to get in all together. There was no soap and she never washed us. Paul would shit in the bathtub and play with it as if they were boats and missiles. Then she would tell us to get out, go get dressed and go to bed. We all smelled like shit. On top of smelling like shit, we would put on dirty clothes. My mother never did the laundry so we would wear the same clothes for days. At this time, I remember my vagina was always sore and swollen from wearing the same underwear for what would seem like months at a time. My butt itched, my feet itched, and my head itched. We had lice.

Aside from the poor hygiene, my mother never took us to the doctor. Her *home remedy* for head lice would be to pour kerosene on our heads. It would burn our scalp and give us sores that lasted forever. The kerosene was so strong at times that it would make our hair fall out. The neglect at this point was pretty bad. My mother even stopped cooking and the refrigerator seemed to always be empty. This apartment only had windows in the kitchen. Most of the time, we didn't have electricity. We rarely saw any daylight.

Annmarie came home crying hysterically one day. She told my mother that Samantha had just died. I remember hugging her and crying. Annmarie's aunts and uncles made all the arrangements for the funeral while all her older siblings were responsible of taking care for the younger siblings. In time, that would soon change. Annmarie took her mother's death very hard and I noticed that she began to drink more. In some ways, my mother seemed happy that Samantha was dead. She always fought with Annmarie when she told her she wanted to spend time Samantha. Soon enough, I'd understand Annmarie and my mother's dynamic more clearly.

I had to adjust to my mother being out all the time. Her absence made me more conscious of what I needed. Fear became obsolete. So did hunger. Many other emotions and feelings that most children should have were altered for me by this point. I needed to be fed, loved, told to focus on school and learn from those around me. Instead, the knocks came on the door. It was the landlord collecting the rent (that she never paid).

On a Monday morning, the knock came on the door and of course, Peter opened it. Standing at the door was the City Marshall who came to evict us. He said we had thirty minutes to take what we could and everything else would go into a city storage unit (until the back rent was paid off). My mother began to get herself dressed. She did her hair without much worry. She then told us to get dressed and made us pack clothes in trash bags. My brothers and I tried to pack up all our little toys and clothes but she began screaming at us. "Don't take anything but clothes!" she yelled. I remember I was crying because I only had one doll and although she was missing a leg, she was my all-time favorite. My mother insisted that I couldn't take her. We all walked out the door. We kept asking our mother where we were going and what would happen to our things. She would just tell us to shut up and keep walking. She never did tell us what would happen to our belongings. I believe this is when my mind began to disassociate itself from being attached to places and things.

We walked to my grandmother's house because we had nowhere to live. My grandmother barely had space for all of us and it seemed as though within a few days, she told my mother we had to leave. She was not nice to us during our whole stay there. My grandmother was only nice to Bippy. I wished that she would care for us as she cared for the baby but I was still happy that Bippy was cared for. My grandmother tells us that she wants us out by the end of the week. She tells us to leave Bippy so Annmarie agrees to let her keep the baby there. At this point, I learned to hate my grandmother the same way she hated us.

We ended up moving in with Jean after we left my grandmother's house. She lived above a funeral home, which creeped out my brothers and I. We would always try to scare each other because we thought dead people were in the hallways. Soon enough, it was back to the same scenario which was drinking, smoking, and strangers sleeping over. We were left alone constantly but this time it was worse. Due to the fact that we were still new to the neighborhood, we never felt safe going outside.

Although my father was still coming by to take us out on Sundays, my mother insisted on asking him to take us to live with him. He refused to take us since he still lived with his mother and there was no room for us. At that time, we thought our father was "the best in the world" so we didn't understand that he could have actually taken us in but simply *chose* not to. This shifted how I felt about my father. I became very angry for the first time with him when he wouldn't take us to live with him.

After about a month of living with Jean, my mother tells us that we are moving again. This time, it was to Ridgewood, Queens on Myrtle Avenue. She also tells us Jean would not be coming with us. We never saw Jean after this and I was glad. There was so much violence between them that it was terrifying. I don't visually remember much of this apartment but I do remember it was on the top floor. The landlord was an old, crazy lady who used to run around the hallway screaming all day. We didn't see many of the same people from Greenpoint. The only person who would come to our house regularly would be Annmarie. She would always bring my mother money. When she would visit, my mother would always drink with her even though she was still young. I began to see my mother having the same type of relationship with her that she had with Jean. They argued about the same things. It was always about money and they physically fought. However, I never saw them being intimate aside from just a simple kiss.

Things at Annmarie's home were rough. The older siblings were having a hard time caring for their younger siblings. Between work, school, and the military for the older siblings, Annmarie was left to do it all. She eventually asked my mother if some of the children could move in. My mother agreed and three of her siblings moved in. I wasn't sure why my mother agreed to take in these children when she never took care of her own but oddly enough, life seemed to get better for a while. Annmarie's siblings became a great addition to the family because Annmarie would cook, clean and care for the family every single day. Annmarie was accustomed to taking care of her siblings since her father was constantly ill until the time of his death. It was the first time I felt like someone genuinely cared for me. She took us to the doctors. She made sure we ate She took care of us as though we were her own. At the time, I thought of her as my hero.

In this apartment, there were eight children and one adult living in just four rooms. I was older now and knew how much drinking was going on but had no power to change it. I understood life was about surviving at this point. Annmarie began drinking just as much as my mother and although she was still trying to care for us, the alcohol was winning. My mother began to send her and Bob out to steal things to get money. They would rob people, stores... pretty much anything. She would also send them out shoe shining. The money would go straight into my mother's hands. Annmarie and my mother were going out to the bars on a regular basis. Annmarie would even steal from the customers at the bars to have enough money to support my mother's drinking habit.

With the both of them out all the time, my brother, Bob was left to watch us. He was not able to do this well. This is when my need to find ways to take care of us began. Bob and I would go shoe shining until late hours of the night just to have money to feed ourselves. They would all stay home alone. On the nights that we would get back home and my mother would be there, my mother would always take the money we earned for herself. We never spent the money until we got home. The thought of doing anything she didn't like frightened us deeply. We spent a lot of time hungry, alone, and walking from bar to bar trying to find my mother and Annmarie. My brothers began going out on their own to steal food and money. Everyone except for Samantha's kids became very self-reliant and began developing skills for survival.

Once again, the knock came at the door. The City Marshall is back. We have thirty minutes to take what we can and leave. This time around there are eight children, three of which have no idea what is going on and begin crying hysterically. The house is in total chaos at this point. My brothers and I give each kid a bag and tell them to fit whatever they can in them. That's all we can take. Everyone is screaming by now. By the tender age of eight, my mind is already disconnected from my surroundings. I'm not crying. I'm not scared. I'm already fearless. I begin to help the other children deal with the reality of what is happening. I no longer have a connection to things I own. They mean nothing. Still, I try to help the other kids pack their bags because I also understand the reality of what thirty minutes means.

We walk out the door with our bags and our mother decides to take us to the bar a few blocks away since she knows the bartender. He is like an uncle to her. As soon as we get there, my mother tells him we've just been evicted and that the landlord was crazy. Of course, she fails to mention she never paid rent. By chance, one of his patrons has an available apartment a few doors away. He then calls the landlord and asks if it's still available. I clearly recall my mother talking to the landlord when he arrives at the bar. All of us sat at the back of the bar waiting while on our best behavior. At this age, we are still scared of my mother so we listened and behaved. She leaves to go see the apartment and the landlord agrees to have us live there. Since she has no way of paying, "Uncle" agrees to lend her the money.

Just like that, we have another apartment. This time it's above a chocolate shop. This apartment was huge and had a lot of rooms. We didn't have any furniture. Just the bags we came in with. We didn't have blankets to sleep on so we just slept on our bags. Over the next few weeks, my brothers, Annmarie, and I would pick up furniture off the street. Of course, my mother was the first one to get a mattress. Over time, we had a mattress on the floor, a table, chairs and other miscellaneous furniture in the house. We had no toys, no books, and no games. There were no children's items whatsoever. As time went on, it started looking like a home. Yet it never really felt like one.

My mother and Annmarie kept drinking a lot. If and when something was cooked, it was always Annmarie's doing. The kids always ate things like *Hamburger Helper* and hot dogs while my mother ate steak! Up until this point in my life, I had never seen my mom cook a meal. She would always talk about what she knew how to cook yet she never once made it for us. It was always *drunken talk*. That's what I called it. Always repeating the same story over and over: every time they drank. Living like this was not easy but oddly enough, the worst part was being kids and living above a chocolate shop. All day long we would smell chocolate. Of course, it wasn't long until my brothers and I figured out a way to get to the chocolate. The chocolate was made indoors and placed on cooling trays in the backyard. We would climb down the fire escape into the yard. Since the fire escape wasn't low enough to reach the candy, I would grab one of them by the ankles and lower him down so he could reach the trays. We'd steal all the chocolate. It was *so good*. I can still sense the scent of that chocolate every time the memory comes back. We did get caught eventually. The store owner told my mother so we had to stop.

Our misadventures were various forms of stealing and finding new ways to make money for our mother. Apart from shoe shining and stealing, my mother had another wonderful trade for us to do. Around the holidays, she would make Annmarie take all the kids and go from bar to bar and sing Christmas carols with a collection can. We'd start early in the day to get to the customers that went to bars during the day. Then we would have to go back out at night to get the customers who were drunk. They always seemed to give us more money. We looked like homeless kids. I guess they felt sorry for us. Still, we were not allowed to touch the money. We would have to bring it straight to my mother every time. Everything done for her and we still wouldn't eat the entire day. Even when we brought her the money, she at most gave us a total of two dollars.

My mother had a way of making everybody do exactly what she wanted, especially Annmarie. She was young and naïve and although I had already seen my mother and her kiss pleasantly on the lips, I never thought anything of it. It was almost like mother and daughter kissing each other. Until the night I awoke to the sounds of moaning. Unaware of what this was, I walk into my mother's bedroom. There I find Annmarie, nineteen at the time, between my mother's legs. I screamed for them to stop. I yelled at my mother, "What are you doing to her!? She's just a kid! You're not supposed to do that to her!" Then I ran back to my bed and cried until I fell asleep. It was at this point that I realized that my mother had been abusing Annmarie from a very young age. She had manipulated her to steal and get money for her. The way I now understood she used her was incredibly sad and conflicting for me. Annmarie was very good to us. Although I was young, I felt very bad for Annmarie. I felt like my mother had taken her and her siblings in just for the money from welfare. Pretty much to mold a young mind and body for her psychopathic needs.

The next day came and my mother acted like nothing happened. Being that she still had a lot of control over me, I didn't bring it up. But I knew. And she knew that I knew. My feelings towards my mother changed dramatically. I saw her as a rapist. Not really understanding everything at the time but I was aware that what she was doing was bad and was not supposed to happen. Life continued in its usual pattern of struggle. We always went back to our job of supporting my mother by shoe shining and stealing. I guess we were just trying to make her happy.

~*~

Now if I thought things were bad before, it was about to get worse. I'm nine years old now. I wake up one morning and as I walk through the rooms, I notice a magazine on the floor. Not knowing what it was, I pick it up and look at the picture carefully. It was a naked man with a hat on his penis. It's a dirty magazine. Along comes Annmarie's brother, Dick. He's fifteen years old at the time. He sees the magazine in my hands and tells me he's going to tell my mother. I tell him he better not. He then yells, "Let me see that and I won't tell", while pointing towards my vagina. I suddenly become very afraid. I don't want him to tell on me. I didn't want my mom to get mad. I shyly agree, not knowing where this was headed. With nobody home at the time, Dick takes me in the bathroom and tells me to pull down my pants. He looks at it. I pull my pants up. "You saw it now", I exclaimed, "don't tell my mother". He then becomes persistent. "No, let me smell it," he replied. I say no. He insists he will tell my mother. I let him smell it. Dick gets down on his knees and sticks his nose in my vagina. He lets me leave the bathroom. I assume it's over.

It doesn't end there. In the weeks following, Dick would make me let him see my vagina and smell it. He always insisted that he would tell my mother if I didn't. I began finding ways not be home alone with him. But life didn't work out that way for me. My brothers were constantly out doing anything to survive. It escalated from seeing and smelling my vagina to sticking his fingers inside it on a daily basis. Sometimes, it was for hours at a time. Always in the bathroom. After about a year of this going on and nobody catching him (and me clearly being too afraid to tell my mother) we moved again.

Now we are back in Greenpoint, Brooklyn. This set up is different in that we had two small three-room apartments across the hall from each other on the fourth floor. I figured I was finally safe from Dick's abuse. Girls are on one side and the boys on the other. Boy, was I wrong! The abuse somehow seems to get worse in this apartment. Nobody was ever home. Dick had total control over me. He took me to school. He watched me from the window playing at lunch time in the yard. He was right outside the gate when I got out of school. Always there to make sure I went home with him. Fear had become a part of me. It was an unknown fear. That's the best way I can describe it.

He has now advanced his abuse towards me. He would stick his fingers in my vagina and my butt and stand there and smell it. It was the weirdest, scariest thing to watch. He would lick my vagina and my butt for what felt like hours, and probably was. He would always try to force my hand on his penis but I would never do it. To this day, it is unclear to me whether he ever penetrated me.

A child's mind has a very particular way of storing the most painful of memories. I was distorted. Although I cannot remember if he actually raped me, his actions definitely raped my soul.

I desperately began finding ways to avoid Dick because he soon became violent. Every time I walked out the door with my mother, he would get mad. Every time I was alone, Dick would start pinching me really hard on the inside of my arm. He began pushing me around the house. The sexual abuse became more violent and forceful. He began to make me touch his penis and hold it. His aggressiveness is getting worse. I began feeling like I had no one to protect me. No one was ever home. I began to leave school from a different door than where Dick would wait and spent my days roaming the streets. This worked for a little while, till it became cold outside. His pinching and pushing only became worse.

One final day, Dick drags me through three rooms by my hair to the bathroom again. Just as we reached the bathroom door (which was next to the front door) my mother walked in. From the look on my face, she knew something was going on. She asked me what happened and I told her the whole story. I told her everything Dick had done to me for the past two and a half years. All at once, my brothers came home and all hell broke loose.

My three brothers beat him down the four flights of stairs. I wasn't sure what was going on in the hallway but I knew it wasn't good. My mother was hitting Annmarie and they began to fight throughout the whole apartment. I never understood why my mother hit Annmarie. It was not her fault; she didn't do it. All my mother kept saying was, "Your brother's a pig! Your brother's a fuckin' pig! He raped my daughter! He raped my daughter!"

All of a sudden, Annmarie (not wanting to hit my mother) punches the glass door and injures her hand badly. There was blood everywhere. I tried to wrap her hand in a towel but I couldn't make it to stop bleeding. My brothers were still in the hallway beating up Dick. I kept telling them to stop because we needed an ambulance for Annmarie. They dragged Dick back into the apartment and we called the ambulance for Annmarie.

Her injury required surgery on her hand. They put a permanent wire in to replace tendons that she had broken. While she was at the hospital, my mother called Annmarie's other siblings to come and pick up the rest of their siblings. My mother didn't want any of them there anymore. As they were taking the kids, my mother kept screaming and going on about everything that happened. As if that wasn't enough, my mother went out the window and screamed it for everyone to hear. I thought at that point my mother would take some responsibility of this being her fault because she was supposed to be the one protecting me. She never did. Once again, life was everybody else's fault.

My mother takes no regard to the situation. She doesn't take me to the doctor. She doesn't even ask me how I am. After all of that, she leaves the house, goes to the bar and leaves me home alone, again. As she walks out the building, my mother continues to tell everyone what just happened. She's already drunk and so loud that I can hear her all the way upstairs. There was no sense of privacy for me since she was always more concerned about people feeling sorry for her than actually being concerned for my wellbeing.

I didn't want to go outside. I was so embarrassed. I felt like it was all my fault since my mother never told me otherwise. Not a hug, nor a kiss. Not an "I'm sorry". Nothing.

By this point, I felt worse than before. I looked out the window and everybody stared at me. I became overwhelmed with emotion. I rushed to the bathroom and opened the medicine chest. I grabbed a bottle of pills. I didn't know what they were. I took all fifteen or twenty of them and laid down, hoping that I would die. I wanted to escape the pain that I was feeling. I felt some peace but sadly, a few hours later, I woke up and spent the next two days puking. No one ever realized what I did. No one seemed to care.

I didn't see Annmarie for about two weeks. I wanted to tell her that I was sorry about telling on her brother and that I never meant for my mother to hit her. I couldn't help but feel guilty. A couple weeks later Annmarie came walking up the block. I was so happy to see her. She still had some kind of cast on her hand. I immediately ran up to her to give her a big hug. I told her how sorry I was for what happened to her. She sat on the stoop with me and told me it wasn't my fault. She insisted that Dick was wrong in his actions and he should have never done that to me. She told me she was sorry. At this moment, I realized how much I loved Annmarie and how important she was in my life. Annmarie made up for the love that my mother never gave me. I needed her to be in my life.

Annmarie came back to live with us and it seemed like my mother had a new way of manipulating her. My mother would not stop making her feel bad for what Dick had done. She would demand more out of her. Annmarie would go out for what seemed like hours and come back with a large sum of money for my mother. They'd always end up using it to go out to the bars.

There were times when Annmarie would bring home random men and lure them to the bedroom as though she was going to sleep with them (by taking off their clothes). Once they were caught off guard, she would take their wallets and run out the door. Being that she was drunk, Annmarie never seemed to realize that I was home in the next room. After hearing the door slam, I'd come out to see what was going on. I'd usually find naked men, who would then chase me around the apartment and try to molest me. This happened so many times that I never truly felt safe in my own house. I was deeply traumatized from all of the sexual abuse I'd been through by now. Yet there was never anybody to help me.

My mother's continuous sexual relationship with Annmarie was also traumatizing. She would have sex with Annmarie knowing that her children could hear her and did not care. My mother would tell us that we were jealous of her. The physical violence between them was always present. Sometimes they would go out with different people only to come home and fight about it all night.

~*~

While my mother and Annmarie lived their lives, my three brothers and I robbed every food factory in the neighborhood. Sometimes we would eat pickles for weeks. We would also rob the pie factory and eat pies until we threw up. By this point, daily life was beyond tough and it felt like hell. To make things worse, the electricity got turned off often or the gas would be off. When both the electricity and the gas would go off it obviously made life impossible.

The house was beyond filthy at this point. My mother never bought us any clothes. The only one that ever bought us clothes was our father and it wasn't much.

Being that our mother never washed our clothes, they would usually end up rotting somewhere on the floor in the apartment. It became so bad that I began going to the laundromat to sit and watch people as they did their laundry. I would wait for them to leave and proceed to steal their clothes from the dryers. As for shoes, we never owned our true size. Everything was too small for our feet. My feet were in so much pain and so itchy that the skin would peel right off.

My mother insisted Annmarie wash her polyester clothes by hand and hang it to dry. She always raved about her figure before she had her children but I never saw it. She once told me that when she was nineteen she had a gum infection that required the dentist to remove all of her teeth. They removed the top row but she never went back for the bottom because "the surgery was too painful". I learned that a lot of my mother's stories were lies she told to make herself look good.

My mother acted as though she didn't have any children. Even when Bob came to live with us, she didn't express any remorse to him. He was just another source of income for her. That's why I was glad when he started dating some girl from New Jersey. After a few months of dating, she convinced him to move to Jersey to start a life together. Of course, my mother was pissed because one of her "fuckin' money makers" was now gone but I was very happy for him. Bob was so miserable at home. My mother was so mad that on their wedding day, she stood up to object their marriage (which pissed everyone off). Despite her complaints, they still got married.

With Bob no longer around, it was just my two brothers and I. Many times Bob and his wife would pick us up and bring us to their house. But we were not good kids. We cursed, we spit, and we stole. We broke shit in their house. We were animals. My brother and his wife could not handle us. They tried to keep us but eventually they'd take us home. We always caused too much trouble for them with their landlord. However, I thank them for trying to help us when no one else would.

My grandmother stopped bringing Bippy over to Annmarie as soon as she found out what happened with Dick. Bippy was a sweet little girl and was always nice. She had the cutest little voice (which sounded like a mouse). She used to bring us candy treats in her snack bag. Out of anger, I used to take the whole bag. It made me really mad that no one took care of us. I would yell at her: "Fuck you! My grandmother takes care of you!" This would always make her cry. I never knew why I took my anger out on her. I guess I was a kid myself.

I would visit my grandmother's house often to see and play with Bippy. Although my grandmother hated me, she would still allow me to play with her. I would run errands for my grandfather Charlie and he would give me a couple of quarters. He was always nice to me. One day while I was there, he tells me that I have another brother named Anthony. After my mother left her first three children, she met Anthony's father and planned on starting a new life with him. However, after Anthony was born, she found out that his father had a few wives. Once again, she walks out leaving Anthony behind with the father.

After this news, I couldn't comprehend what I was hearing or where these kids were at the moment. There was never any talk of Anthony or any of her other children. I never noticed my mother making any attempts at reaching out to them. They became obsolete in my life; never knowing them or understanding what had become of their lives or where they were... It was as if they never existed. When would my mother do the same to us?

Daily life was just that: survival at its fullest. Learning and discovering more ways to steal. Only to once again come home from school to find the City Marshall truck in front of our building. It took me a moment to realize what was going on. I looked up and saw a large drop chute coming from our 4th floor window. Officials were throwing all our belongings down the chute and into the truck. I immediately became incredibly embarrassed; all the neighbors were outside watching it happen. I turned around and walked the other way. What little I had to wear was now being thrown away like yesterday's trash. All I really owned were two pair of pants, one skirt, and two shirts. Now all I was left with was the clothes on my back. I head to the bar to tell my mother. She had no reaction. When I looked down, I noticed my mother had a bag of her clothes beside her. That's when I realized she already knew what was happening. Selfish Cunt.

Now my mother, Annmarie, Peter, Paul and I are homeless with nowhere to go. I remember feeling utterly hopeless. Even though our former apartment felt like hell, at least we had a place to call home. Now we had nothing. My mother didn't seem to be affected by the changes. She continued her days as though nothing ever happened. We would just walk from bar to bar hoping we'd find her and she'd give us money for food. Instead she would tell us to leave the bar and go "play at the park". We would run the streets all hours of the day and night and slept in the back of bars, amidst the booths or on the filthy floors.

Here, I was awoken on multiple nights by strange men touching my vagina and sticking their tongues in my mouth. I can still remember the stench and taste of their beer and cigarettes in my mouth. They would tell me how pretty I was. When I'd scream, most of them would get away from me. But some of them wouldn't. Some would stay until my brother's got up and hit them with whatever they found lying around the back: spare chairs, Christmas décor, etc. Then the creeps would run out. All the while, my mother lay asleep in the next booth. Never caring or recognizing her daughter's cries. Even when I'd tell her what happened and pointed out one of these men she would simply use it to her advantage: to get money for drinks from them. The men would give the same excuse every time: they were drunk and "didn't realize what they were doing". Never giving a fuck. Never truly giving a shit about me.

After about two weeks of sleeping in bars, my mother decides to bring us to my grandmother's house so that she can watch us "for a little while". After about four or five days, my mom shows up and my grandmother tells us she wants us out of her house. My mom tells us she is going to the store and disappears again. My grandmother goes out to find her and tell her that if she doesn't pick us up, she'll take us down to ACS to put us in foster care. My mother never returns to my grandmother's to pick us up.

The next morning, my grandmother wakes up and she takes us down the ACS office. She walks in with us and tells a woman at the desk that she can no longer take care of us and does not know where our mother is. The woman bursts into frantic questioning about how she is related to us and my mother's whereabouts. After what seemed like forever, my grandmother stands up and starts walking towards the door with Bippy. What I recall the most about that moment is Bippy saying, "I'll see you later Donna". She had no idea what was going on. Bippy was used to leaving us and going home with my grandmother but little did she know she would never see us again. My grandmother didn't even say goodbye. I had so much hatred for my mother and grandmother at this point. All at once, I was terrified of not knowing what exactly was going on. To top it all off, this all happened the day before my twelfth birthday.

~*~

We're left at this agency and are taken into an office. I remember being asked a lot of questions about what life was like for us. I would answer all the questions. I never said anything bad about my mother. I just wanted to go home. I felt like I was more of a mom to my brothers than anyone so naturally I wanted to protect them. No matter what it was when it came to them I always took care of it. When food was involved I made sure they ate first. We just wanted to get out of there. We were all so skinny and malnourished. We were dirty and our hair was full of lice. It was matted to our heads. I could overhear adults saying things to each other like, "oh my God! How did these children survive?" Not knowing the difference, I didn't even care how bad home was; at this moment it was all I wanted. As I sat there in the office looking for ways to escape, I realized the door was locked and we were not getting out.

"What's happening? Can we go home?" She begins to explain to me what ACS is and what they're going to do for us. She tells me they're going to find us a place to live. But first off, they need to take us to the hospital to get physical examinations done to make sure we're healthy enough to be placed in someone's home. Although thin and unkempt, we are able to be placed in someone's home. We head back to the agency and I immediately tell the lady I need to be with my brothers. She tells me she will only be able to keep us together if she can find a home that will take all three of us. If not, we would unfortunately have to be separated. I began experiencing extreme panic and my mind was racing at the mere thought of not seeing my brothers again. I thought of all the other siblings I had out in the world somewhere that I never got to know. Peter and Paul were all I had at the moment and this seemed like the end of what little family I had.

After what seemed like hours, the case worker came back and said she found a woman that would take all three of us. She told us it would only be temporary: till they found us a more permanent home. We didn't know what to think at that moment. We no longer had a home. We had no belongings. At least we had each other.

We arrived at the house and as the door opened a short woman, about 45 years old, stepped out. She stared at us with a look I had never seen before. We went inside and she introduced herself to us as Laura and her husband as Steve. She had a dog named Pepper and three cats, one of them whom was large and named Candy (the other cat's names I can't recall). We were all scared. My brothers stood behind me the whole time. Laura offered us food. Once we were done, she insisted we get some rest and talk more in the morning. Laura had a separate room upstairs for me and wanted the boys to sleep downstairs with the other two foster kids (who were also boys). When my brothers heard this, they immediately broke into tears. I asked her if they could sleep upstairs with me and told her I would convince them to sleeping downstairs the following night. Laura agreed and all three of us slept upstairs in a twin bed. We were so exhausted; we passed out as soon as our heads hit the pillows.

The next morning we woke up to the smell of food cooking which was not normal for us. I asked my brothers if they were hungry and they both said yes. I told them, "Come on, let's go!" but they were scared. I decided to cough so Laura knew we were awake. She instinctively came and knocked on the door. I opened it. She took us to the bathroom and gave us tooth brushes and washcloths and told us to "brush our teeth and clean our faces so we could eat breakfast". "After breakfast," she said, "we're gonna go buy some clothes." My brothers and I simply looked at each other in shock.

We finished eating and Laura took us to the store. She asked us for our sizes but we had no idea. Laura picked out some clothes and we tried them on to find our correct sizes. She bought us everything from underwear to jackets. It was more than I ever owned at once. This was amazing to us but terrifying to me at the same time. I couldn't understand why she was being so nice to us.

I was very quiet for the first few days, absorbing my surroundings. I couldn't believe how this woman lived. The house was always impeccably clean, there was food and the lights were always on. She told us "if you're thirsty, help yourself to something to drink," yet we wouldn't dare go anywhere near the refrigerator. It took us a while to warm up to Laura and Steve but out of the three of us Paul was the first. He was the youngest and the most trusting. It would take Peter and I much longer. Peter would usually wait for me to take the lead and then he would follow. My brothers both trusted me because I made sure to always keep them safe.

After about nine days, Laura tells us we'll be leaving the next morning. Laura explains to me that she was the type of foster parent that only held children temporarily. Until the agency found permanent homes for the kids she took in. I was so mad at this point, I started thinking, "now she doesn't even want us! Where are we going to go now?" I began to panic at the thought of what the case worker originally told me. *The ACS might not be able to find a home for all three of us and will have to separate us.* The next morning comes and the case worker is at the door. As we say our goodbyes, I could not help but cry. We had finally started feeling comfortable. I asked if we could take the clothes Laura bought for us. They agreed. Laura gave us a big hug and we left. I kept wondering what would be next.

~*~

The first question I asked the case worker was if my brothers and I would be staying together. She tells me she has found a woman that will take all three of us in. I was so relieved. They took us to our new foster home where a woman by the name of Bee greets us. She already had a bunch of her own children. Bee ran a business out of her unfinished basement making ceramics. She seemed to be nice while the case worker was there but as soon as she left, Bee was horrible to us. She made us sleep in the basement on cots even though she told the ACS worker that we would be sleeping in the bedrooms upstairs. I couldn't even tell you what one of those rooms looked like because we never even saw them. We never even spoke to Bee while we were living there. We didn't like staying with her one bit.

After a few weeks, the case worker came to check on us and I told her what was really going on. She was clearly very upset. What I didn't know at the time was that she actually was coming to tell us that Laura wanted us back at her house. As soon as I heard the news, I was thrilled. For the first time in my life it felt like someone actually cared. Even though I was still a little wary, I was relieved.

We packed our belongings and headed back to Laura's house. I remember the anticipation I felt at the thought of seeing her again. I couldn't believe it was real. I was always the type of person that needed to have proof in order to believe something. When we got there, Laura opened the door and we all hugged. I remember thanking her and the look on her face was again, one I was not used to. It made me feel something inside that I had never experienced before. But it felt good. I remember asking her, "When will we have to leave again?" Laura told me we were there to stay.

Laura was such a kind and generous woman. She enrolled us in school immediately. She was a no-nonsense kind of woman. She let us know up front what was expected of us and how much she wanted us to do well. And I believed her.

I had plenty of clothes to wear now. More than I could ever imagine. And so many pair of panties! It felt so good not to have to wear the same panties for weeks at a time. The rashes between my legs went away. My skin glowed and my hair stopped failing out. My shoes fit and my feet weren't in constant pain anymore. All these changes seemed weird to me.

I was in school. I had friends. I was learning how to be a normal kid. I began swimming and going to the park with Laura. I loved playing tackle football and gained plenty of bumps and bruises from it. Laura took care of all of them. She wasn't like my mother at all. It seemed too good to be true. It was as if I was living someone else's life. Somehow through it all I still wanted to be back with my mother. I missed her a lot.

We didn't get to see her often. At most I'd see my mother once a month. We would have to travel to Jamaica, Queens to visit her at the foster care agency. Her visits were always supervised. Sometimes we would get there and she wouldn't even show up. We'd always end up in tears on our way back to Laura's.

After about a year of living there, Paul stole a dollar from Laura's drawer and blamed it on Peter. Laura believed him and sent Peter to live somewhere else. I was clearly upset so Laura promised to let me call him whenever I want. Peter moved to Long Island with another foster family. After his move, I became withdrawn for a couple of weeks, mostly out of anger, but mainly because this was the first time we were ever separated in our lives. Six months pass and Paul steals from Laura again. This time he blames it on me. Once again, Laura believes him but this time she wants *me* to leave. At this point I finally realize that Paul was lying and Peter never stole anything in the first place. I slapped the shit out of him.

The case worker ended up taking me to the home in Long Island where Peter stayed. Unaware that Peter had run away from this foster home (and gone back to live with my mother) I was devastated as soon as I got there and found out the news. I didn't want to stay there at all but I had no choice. This is the first time I am all alone without anyone I actually know. This new reality changed me. Rage has total control over me. A new *me* emerges.

~*~

When I arrive at the Long Island house, I learn the owner lives there with her husband and two grown children of her own. She also had two other foster children at the time: a brother and sister. The woman and her husband were very nice and spoke highly of my brother Peter. They told me they missed him. Their daughter was very nice as well but their son was miserable. He was huge and he was always very mean to the foster kids. I was at their home for about three to four weeks.

One night, I was in bed laughing with the other foster girl. The foster mother's son apparently did not like it so banged on our door while threatening to hit us. I remember he had a big flashlight in his hand that he kept banging on the bedpost. At one point he banged it so hard that the top of the flashlight came off and the glass bulb hit me, cutting my eye. In that instant, I decided I was running away (and the other foster girl wanted to go with me). We went to sleep and when morning came, we both set out on our way. We had no money. We just grabbed the only thing we could which was our lunch bags. I didn't know exactly where I was but I knew which bus route took us from there to Jamaica (back to the agency where I used to visit my mother).

We decided to walk by following the bus route from Hempstead, Long Island to Jamaica, Queens. This took about four hours total. Once we got there, I remembered the bus route that took us from the agency to Laura's house. We then walked the bus route from Jamaica, Queens to Ozone Park. That took us about two hours. Once we arrived at Laura's, I knew how to take the train to my mother's new apartment.

It had been seven hours once we finally arrived to my mother's apartment. When I walk in the door she takes one look at me and with an attitude says, "What are you doing here?!" I couldn't even believe her words. I began to tell my mother about what had happened to my eye. The only thing she said was, "go over to the Ambulance Corp. and check your eye!" Why was I even surprised by now?

I went to the Ambulance Corp. and they told me I had to go to the hospital and my mother had to go with me (since I was still a minor). The doctors removed glass from my eye and bandaged it. They also gave me crutches because they said I strained my ligaments from all the walking. As soon as we get back to my mother's house, she yells, "You know you can't stay here. You have to go back!" Back to foster care. The emptiness and despair was back again. I told my mother to go fuck herself and I left. My mother called ACS and told them what had happened. They came to pick up the other foster girl and took her back to Long Island. But by then, I was already gone.

It was at this moment that I decided death must be better than foster care. I tried to take my own life again. I sat across the street from my mother's house (in the park). I took a dirty piece of glass from the ground and cut my right wrist. It bled a lot. As I sat there, I patiently watched it bleed for a long time. I could hear my mother's laughter from her window in the distance. It infuriated me so much that I said to myself, "you don't win bitch!" I grabbed my sweater to stop the bleeding. I knew I couldn't go to the hospital so I went to a friend's house instead. She cleaned my cut and bandaged it for me. At least I wasn't completely alone.

After leaving my mother's house that day, I basically lived from house to house, running wild on the streets. Peter would come looking for me to go home and I would go back to my mother's house, stay a few days, and leave again. Peter was struggling without me there. He was now more self-reliant and able to take care of himself but still not fully independent at this point. There is still no food in the house. Peter and I would hold sliced bread over the open flame on the stove to cook it and then spread mayonnaise on it. Although food was always scarce, my mother always kept mayonnaise in the fridge. So weird.

~*~

My mother eventually goes to court and gets custody of Paul and I back (most likely for the welfare money). My mother and Annmarie were still drinking heavily from bar to bar. Nothing had changed from the time I left to foster care. Peter wanted to hit Paul for lying and splitting us up but I would never allow them to hit each other. I felt really bad about it but I began to see my mother's effects on Paul. He was different now. Just like Peter and I, Paul learned his own way of survival.

My mother enrolled all of us in school (mostly due to the fact it was the law). Once the school received my grades from my previous school, I was placed in 8AB, the top class for the 8th grade. I was very smart in school and enjoyed learning. Yet to me, survival always came first. Therefore, school became an option, not a priority. Even in school I would rob the gym lockers for clothes. I also played handball and would make others play me for money. I would *always* win.

I would even rob all the Catholic school girls when they walked from school. They always had money and nice sneakers. Basically, if I needed something I had to steal it. I had no fear of anything at this point. I was so reckless that the thought of going to jail never even crossed my mind. There was nothing and no one that could scare me at this point. At fourteen years of age I just needed to eat and live through another day. I continued to float from house to house. I would drink, smoke pot, use cocaine; anything to escape reality. Although I knew my mother still did not care, I was somewhat hopeful that she would save me and somehow try to make it right. Every day it seemed as though time passed and my waiting was just that. Waiting. I began to feel as though the outside world could see through me so I began to wear a mask of sorts. Simply letting others see what I wanted them to see. I stayed this way for many years.

The environment at my mother's new apartment was the worst of all of them. Perhaps due to the fact I was now older and understood more. There was a kitchen, my room, Peter and Paul's room, and the last room was my mother's and Annmarie's. The house was filthy all the time. Anyone in the neighborhood who was on drugs or in some way intoxicated always ended up at this apartment. My mother was never home but when she was, the constant fighting never seemed to end. The fighting was so bad that they would break all the glass windows out. Since my room was right next to the kitchen, I never slept. The strangers would always try to get into my bed to sleep or God knows what else. Nothing ever seemed to change.

One of the freakiest and most memorable visuals I have of this apartment was the swinging lightbulb. Whenever we had no light my mother would steal electricity by plugging an extension cord into the hallway socket. She would tie the cord to the kitchen ceiling fixture. Talk about creepy. When everyone was drunk, the cigarette smoke and dim light would shade their faces making them look eerie and distorted. That memory will never leave me.

I hung around some of the worst neighborhoods: selling drugs, robbing drug dealers, and thriving off the chaos. Anyone was fair game for me at this point. I hated the world. I would fight at least twice a day and it didn't matter who you were: if you looked at me the wrong way, I just punched the shit out of you. I was robbing and beating people for what I needed every day. Amidst it all, I found myself back at my mother's house every day trying to clean it and checking in on my brothers. By now, smoking marijuana and drinking became an everyday thing for me. I was evolving into everything I despised.

At this time, I mostly dressed in street clothes: baggy jeans, t-shirts... very tomboy-ish. Hanging out on stoops and street corners, drinking a 40 oz of beer and smoking joints was my every day. Just running wild. Until I discovered how I could use my appearance to get what I wanted. Being that I preferred to associate with much older people, I started wearing make-up and began dressing like an adult. Miniskirts and high heels were in fashion and I had the body for it. I also noticed my effect on men and began to understand how I could use it to my advantage. Up until this point, any thought of sexual behavior was sickening to me. Although internally that would not change, I learned how I could utilize it.

I no longer hung out with people my age. My crowd was much older than me. Whether they knew my actual age or not, they never seemed to care. It was repulsive to me how grown men could desire such a young girl. And how easy it was for me to get them to give me whatever I wanted simply with words. No sexual acts whatsoever. I had basically decided I was never having sex. The thought of it disturbed me and these men just confirmed how I felt. I was young enough to be their daughter and they still wanted to fuck me. That's why it never stopped me from taking their money. In a way, their sick behavior made me want to take it more.

I was hanging out in bars. I had all kinds of male friends: cops, firemen, congressmen, married men... all at my disposal. I didn't seem to need much these days. I pretty much had everything I needed. Yet as quick as it came, it would go. I had no regard for money or belongings. I felt I knew how easy it was to get what I needed. I was still drinking and smoking marijuana but now I begin using cocaine on a regular basis. Never having to pay for it made it a whole lot easier to consume every day. My life was spiraling downwards and I didn't care. The drugs seemed to stop my excessive thinking and worrying. For the time being.

One day while eating a slice at Al's Pizzeria, I notice a boy my age staring at me. He is so cute. Something weird happens inside me. Something I had never felt before. Although I'm used to talking to men to get what I need, this feels different. When he comes over to talk to me, he introduces himself politely. He simply glances at me and says, "Hi. I'm Dean. Would you like to go to the movies with me?" and I quickly agree. I was very overwhelmed and confused with how I felt about him. I didn't know if I should trust him. Yet I enjoyed being around him so I continued to date him.

Dean was a good kid who came from a great family. They treated me very well and he did too. I developed many feelings for him but I never understood any of them. The emotions he evoked actually scared me and the love he showed me felt even more terrifying. He took me to the movies, out for pizza, etc. I guess this was normal stuff for teenagers but my world was different. His mom was so nice to me. She was really concerned about me. I loved her for being there for me. Though Dean and I loved each other very much, my life on the streets led to us spending less and less time together. Although I had brought him to my mother's house on several occasions, I was embarrassed every single time. His home was normal compared to mine. I truly believed he deserved better being that he came from a good family. Why should he be with someone like me who has all these problems? It made no sense. When we separated, Dean was utterly heartbroken. I was too but I truly believed life for him would be better this way. We remained friends and would talk often for many years. I missed him for a long time once we lost touch but back then, I could not make a good decision about my life or for myself.

~*~

Back at my mother's hellhole everyone is still fucking nuts. I still visited every day to give my brothers money and food. On hot days, they would take the coffee table and chairs and sometimes the mattresses across the street and have parties while the fire hydrant would be on. The neighbors thought we were insane. Everyone were pretty much scared of us. Most people wouldn't walk under our window because at any given moment someone would be throwing up out of it. Although for most people this would be embarrassing, it was *my normal*. I was immune to worrying about what other people thought.

Even the cops never seemed to care. They would simply drive by and laugh. At no point did they see us kids there and feel sorry for us. It seemed as though throughout the years, no one actually cared. My family was a joke to a lot of people. I guess people figured that if my mom didn't care, why should they? They were right. It's up to the mother to protect you, care for you and nurture you. If she isn't doing these things then why should anyone else?

My father did nothing to help. When we were very young, I thought my father was *the greatest*. But as I got older, I realized he was no better than my mother. He was a sober man who lived a relatively normal life. Yet I never understood how he was able to go home knowing the kind of environment he was dropping us off to. I would cry for hours after he left. He never came back to get us. He *could* have made a difference. He *could* have at least tried. Yet I never found myself asking him why. To this day, I barely speak to the man. I now realize he was just like my mother. Disconnected from how one should care and protect their children.

I'm now living from place to place with girlfriends who are much older than me. Many of them had children. Despite their age (and the fact that they had jobs) the drugs and alcohol prevented them from fully functioning as parents. We drank and did cocaine at all hours of the night. Still, I took care of all the important stuff for their kids, such as taking them to school, cooking, doing their laundry, and cleaning the house. Even though I was doing the same drugs my friends were, I was aware the kids' needs were important. My girlfriends were there for me when I needed them; I knew I had to help them (and their kids) however I could.

While Annmarie and my mother were running from bar to bar, Annmarie's daughter Bippy was living the good life with my grandmother. My grandfather Charlie adored this little girl with every ounce of love you would possibly give a child. Meanwhile, Annmarie is pregnant with her second child and she decides to keep the baby. The second baby was a girl named Maria and she was the prettiest little girl you could imagine. At the time I wasn't living there but I decided to stay because I knew Annmarie would need me to help with the baby. Annmarie loved Maria so much but her alcohol addiction was stronger than she could handle. After about two weeks of Maria being born, Annmarie and my mother were back at the bars leaving me without any diapers or formula. Sometimes I had no choice but to use towels for diapers and hand wash them later.

Over the next eight months, while my mother and Annmarie continue drinking and going to the bars, I cared for Maria by stealing diapers, formula, and baby food from the A&P on the corner. I had never taken care of an infant so it was very scary. There were also no lights in the house at the time which made things much worse. I would always try to put Maria to sleep as soon as it became dark because I didn't want her to strain her eyesight. It was hard but I had to do it because Annmarie had already done so much for my brothers and I.

One night while taking care of Maria, Annmarie leaves the apartment to go buy some diapers. Three hours passes and I decide to go to the bar on Kingsland Avenue to find Annmarie. I would never bring Maria to the bar so I asked a friend to care for her. Since all the neighbors by now knew what was going on, someone decided to call ACS while I was gone. Once I got back from the bar, the cops were already there and as I went to take Maria, I realized that they were there for her. The cops told me not to touch the baby. I told the cops that I was Maria's sister and that her mother was up the block. The cops tell me they know who her mother is. As soon as I turn around, I see Annmarie getting arrested by the cops. I ask them if I can take Maria home. They remind me that I'm only sixteen years old and I'm too young to take care of her.

I asked the cops where they were taking Maria and they told me she would first go to the hospital for a check-up and then to a foster home. I walk to Greenpoint Hospital and sneak in through the emergency room.

From room to room, following her cries, I look for Maria till I find her. She's in a crib and as soon as she sees me, she stops crying and puts her hands out for me to pick her up. Within the minute, a nurse walks in and asks me who I am. I tell the nurse I'm her sister and explained to her what happened. I tell her I've been the one taking care of Maria and how I know I'm not supposed to be there. Then I beg the nurse to please let me change Maria into her pajamas and put her to sleep for the night. The nurse agrees. I change her clothes, give her a bottle and sing her a song till she falls asleep. I go home and the next day Annmarie comes home upset and crying. I told her I was sorry that I failed her and she just said "you did your best. It's okay". She once again insists me it was not my fault.

Over the next few months, Annmarie goes to court to get Maria back. I meet her foster mother, Jenny. She was a very nice lady. Annmarie manages to get custody back of Maria. I will never forget the day she brought Maria back home. I ran to my mother's house as fast as I could to see the baby. I didn't think she would remember me. Yet from the minute Maria saw me, she hugged and kissed me and didn't want anyone else but me. When Jenny was about to leave she asked Annmarie if she could visit the baby sometime. Annmarie agrees. I become upset. There are still no lights in the house, my mother and Annmarie are still drinking heavily. Now they have Maria to take care of (again) which actually means I have to take care of her myself. The relationship between my mother and I had become physically violent at this point making it impossible for me to stay there (much less to care for Maria).

I stay there anyway. Jenny visits regularly during this time and continuously asks Annmarie if she can take Maria home to take care of her. I decide to sit down with Annmarie (who now has learned she is about eight months pregnant) and explain to her why it would be best if Maria lived with the foster mother. Annmarie agrees and Jenny promises to bring Maria anytime Annmarie desires. I still believe that was the smart choice for Annmarie and Maria. The little girl went to live with her foster mother and Annmarie got to see her whenever she wanted. Jenny was a very good person and treated Annmarie the same way.

Annmarie's third pregnancy was rough and lead to her being in constant bedrest for the final two months. It was because of this that Jenny decided to ask Annmarie if she would be interested in giving her newborn to her sister, Carol (who was also a foster parent). Annmarie was quite conflicted and asks me what she should do. I tell her to let Maria and the newborn go with Jenny and Carol, at least until things get better. Alcohol is a funny thing. It has a way of controlling people. Yet things were different for Annmarie. No matter what she went through, Annmarie loved her children and she was never selfish to their needs. Deep down inside, she knew that she couldn't handle it yet she didn't want them to suffer in the process. That's something I will always commend her for.

Annmarie's new baby girl, Susie is born in August. Annmarie was ecstatic; she was proud mother. I could see the love for her children in her eyes, which is something I never experienced as a child. After Susie and Annmarie came back from the hospital, everyone was there to welcome them. Jenny was there with Maria, as were my grandmother and Bippy. My brothers and I were there cleaning the house all day and of course, my mother just sat on her fat ass all day holding the baby. The whole house was packed. We decided Susie would stay home with Annmarie for a while. After a couple of weeks, Annmarie started drinking again so it was time for Susie to go live with Carol. Annmarie's children were blessed with amazing women to care for them. Although they visited often, Maria and Susie led normal lives with people that loved them.

As much as I wanted to care for these children, at this point I myself was losing control. My nights consisted of going to bars, drinking, and ending up at friends' apartments to do drugs until the early morning. Sleeping all day and escaping all night. This was my life now. I knew being high all the time made it unsafe for the kids. It was incredibly hard to see them go but it was the best decision Annmarie could've made.

The only kids who seemed to suffer were my brothers and I but by this time we had learned to be fully self-sufficient. I was still living from one place to another, never knowing a permanent home. Yet this was normal for me. I finished the 9th grade as part of Junior High and graduated but decided not to go to the graduation ceremony. The school board assigned me to Eastern District High School but I never showed up. I just didn't see the point.

I spent so many years as a child embarrassed of having to wear dirty clothes and having bugs in my hair. On top of that I stunk from not bathing. Even if I was a clean kid, I would still feel like people knew about the problems in my personal and home life. I wasn't like most kids. I didn't have dreams of being anything but myself. By the time high school came I was completely out of control. Who has time for school when you have to struggle just to find a place to sleep at night?

My life kept going from bad to worse no matter what I did. I always had a feeling in the back of my mind that I would turn out to be just like my mother. Even though I didn't live at her house, I had this sick need to see her every day. Even if it was just to curse her out (I still had to do it). My pain was unbearable and that was how I dealt with it. My judgement was clouded and I was full of rage, paranoia, and God knows what else.

Paul was still living with my mother and surviving in his own way. He would always help others no matter what. Never asking for anything and always grateful for anything he was given. Even though I didn't live there, I made it my business to make sure he was never hungry. I would bring Paul money. I'd take him out shopping for clothes. I'd pick him up for a slice of pizza whenever I could. It was obvious to me he was having a difficult time without me at my mother's. He would always ask, "Donna, are you gonna stay home tonight?" and I'd always have to lie and tell him I'd be back later.

Meanwhile Peter was working full-time and he was clearly my mother's favorite. I guess it was the forty dollars a week that my mother forced him to pay as "board" that kept her happy. Peter could do no wrong in her eyes. He would act out and do mean shit all the time. Lying to get Paul and I in trouble, stealing whatever he could (still blaming us) and my mother would always believe him. Either I would leave or wait for my mother to leave so I could slap the shit out of him. This was part of my brother's malfunctioning. Peter just wanted me to stay home with them. He would go as far as calling the cops in attempts at getting me to live there. The cops would always tell him, "She doesn't have to stay here" and leave. I ultimately believe this is what made him react and do the things he did. Russell Street is forever scarred by my family living there.

~*~

One December night in 1984, I was hanging out with two girlfriends at their apartment drinking some beers and listening to music, laughing, and dancing. While tripping on acid, we decided to do a few lines of cocaine (which was normal for us). The partying continued till dawn but the coke ran out. We called everyone we knew trying to score but nobody answered. Suddenly we remembered the guy next door was a dealer. We knocked on his door. He told us he only had "pure" cocaine and nothing to cut it with. Being so high we didn't care and took it anyway.

We continued to get high. Out of nowhere my nose started to bleed. When the left nostril bled, I'd sniff the coke into the right side. When the right nostril bled... you get the picture. At about eight in the morning, I leave their apartment and head to my friend Melody's house (where I've been living at the time). As soon as I get to my room, I lay down on the cot and closed my eyes. Instantly, I projectile vomit straight up into the air. It doesn't stop. The vomit falls back on my face and chest so I somehow throw myself off the bed and onto the floor.

I thought that I was dying. I was too sick to get up. I even peed on myself. It took me five days just drag myself from the floor and back onto the cot. It was always useless since I always ended up on that floor again. Lying there smelling like vomit and piss made the nausea unbearable. A week passed and I couldn't even get myself to the bathroom for a shower. I was extremely weak from not eating and just puking bile. I was dealing with this all alone. Although Melody tried to help take care of me, she insisted I should go to the hospital but I always refused.

One more week passed and I decided to go to my mother's apartment. For some crazy reason, I thought that if anyone would understand or try to help, it would be her. My legs were shaking so bad that it took me about two hours just to walk three and a half blocks. I was sweating profusely and vomiting all the way there. Once I finally made it to my mother's, I felt a sense of relief. I really didn't want to tell her what had happened. But at the same time, I knew there was no other choice. I just blurted it out. Her response: "I don't help drug addicts" and she threw me out.

I was shocked. I could not believe my own mother would do that to me. The bitch ruined my life and wouldn't even try to make up for it. As if she was the best of mothers. I should've known better than to go to her. A perfect stranger would have done more for me. I left and went back to Melody's. Eventually I got better with time. It was after this incident that I decided I would never do hard drugs again.

Over the next six months, I still drank and smoked weed but no cocaine or acid. After my overdose I was afraid to touch cocaine. Even though I was grateful to be alive, I don't think I actually knew what that meant.

~*~

On July 5th, I woke up with a toothache. I went to my mother's house to ask for my Medicaid card and if she could go to the dentist with me. Uncertain of where to go, I figured my mother would take me this time. My mother was just waking up. For my mother, "just waking up" meant sitting on the toilet for three hours shitting and smoking cigarettes. She'd then have a couple of drinks and decide how her day would go. As I sat at the kitchen table waiting for her, the pain in my mouth was getting worse by the minute. After all that waiting, she refused to take me. She simply told me to put a little scotch on my finger and rub it onto my gums.

My mother leaves and I sit in the kitchen for about five hours (while putting Scotch on my gums and taking some Tylenol pills I managed to get from a neighbor). When my mom finally comes back home I ask her to take me to the dentist once again (probably out of desperation). As usual, she asks Annmarie to take me instead. Even though Annmarie was usually the one who would take us to the doctor, she was drunk this time and refused. It was nighttime so the dentist office was already closed. The only place left to go was the emergency room. After another hour of begging and crying to my mother, I began having stomach pains. I assumed it was from all the crying from my toothache. My mother finally called the ambulance and off we went.

At the hospital, my mother sits beside me and holds my hand (only to keep up the appearance of being a caring and loving mother) as the doctor walks in. I tell him about my toothache and mention my "stomach is really hurting". He tells me the oral surgeon is not available but he will be taking some of my blood and urine, as well as examine me vaginally to see what the stomach pains were about. I tell him that I had been crying for the past ten hours and assume it's from that. He still insists on giving me a vaginal examination "to make sure everything is okay".

The doctor proceeds to examine me. I'm incredibly uncomfortable. It's very painful. Once he is finished, he tells me to get dressed and walks out. I get up from the examination table only to discover blood everywhere. I clean myself up, terrified, and get dressed. As soon as the doctor comes back in I yell at him, "What the fuck is that?" pointing to the blood. "What the fuck did you do to me?" I exhale, "I didn't come in here bleeding!" He asks me for my name is and tells me to take a seat. The doctor insists everything is fine. He tells me the bleeding is from having a pelvic examination at 19.3 weeks and it will stop shortly.

I ask him what he's talking about and what those numbers mean. The doctor repeats himself, "the bleeding was from the examination because you are 19.3 weeks". I have no idea what he's talking about. I ask him to explain his words one more time. He then comes to the realization that I had no idea I was pregnant. I'm in disbelief. I tell him he must be wrong because my period came every month. Just as I'm telling him this, the blood and urine tests come back and confirm his words. "I can't have the baby" I exclaim to him, "and I need to get an abortion". He said this was not an option since I was already five months pregnant. I was devastated.

Here I am: pregnant, homeless and looking for answers. After the hospital I went back to my mother's house and stayed there while looking for a place to have an abortion. Each time I was turned away with the explanation of it "being too late". Eventually I realized I had no choice but to keep the baby.

My concern for my baby at this point was incredibly overwhelming. Confused and not knowing exactly what to do, I turned to my mother in hopes that she would help me through the pregnancy. I moved back into her apartment but she continued to live the same lifestyle; never showing an ounce of concern. She didn't even care if I ate. Like usual, there were not even lights on in the apartment.

From the day I found out I was pregnant something changed in me: I was in a fog. I didn't want to go outside. I'm not sure if it was my nerves or if I was scared of something in particular but I always felt like something bad was going to happen to me. I would just sit in my mother's apartment day and night. In the dark! The dysfunction I was used to became surreal to me. It was almost as though I was waking up and seeing my life for what it really was.

Up until this point in my life everything I had done, seen, or lived through I perceived as normal. My mind (damaged from all of it) lead me to begin feeling a sense of reality. It was incredibly petrifying. Consumed by thoughts of having a baby and how I'd care for it, my anxiety begins.

I only had sex two times after Dean and I broke up. Although I had a good idea on who the father was, I was never quite sure.

One guy I had a relationship with for a couple of months. The other guy was a "one time" situation that I cared nothing about. I decided that when my baby was born I would tell him that his father died. I didn't want to complicate anyone else's life. This was my baby.

Over the following months, Peter (who was still living at my mom's) was working a night shift at the time and would bring me food before and after work whenever he had the chance. He and his girlfriend Sofia were pretty much the only ones who fed me. Sofia was always very kind to me. Although she had very little, she would still bring me pizza and sweets whenever she could. I was relieved and thankful because they were there for me when I needed him them the most. I am forever thankful to them for it. They truly helped my baby survive.

My pregnancy didn't start to show until the eighth month. It was a cute little bump. Sadly, I never got to go through any prenatal care. My baby was coming and I had no idea what to do. Sitting in the dark day after day, hungry and withdrawn, it all began to take a toll on me. I had nowhere to turn so I called my father. I asked him for help and he simply replied, "What do you want me to do? I live with my mother!" As usual, he was not available. I decided then and there that *whatever happens will be my destiny*.

About a week later, I was sleeping next to Paul when my water broke. I was so scared that I called out for my mother. She walked right by me and into the bathroom. She couldn't function when she wasn't drunk. Paul helped me change my wet pants and called the ambulance while Annmarie and my mother got ready to leave with me.

I was in labor for six hours. Annmarie was so helpful. She was scared and excited for me all at once, always telling me it would be okay. This helped calmed my nerves a bit, at least until my mother came into the room. My mother started stealing nail polish remover pads and yapping her ass off to everyone. The room I was in had the storage closet so every time a staff member came in, not only would she try to steal more bandages and supplies, she would also lift up the blanket and show off my bare ass with the baby coming out. I couldn't believe it. I later found out Annmarie was giving Vodka shots to the other pregnant women in the waiting room. Fucking straight crazy.

With three pushes my son, Dino, was born. I couldn't believe I was a mother. He was so beautiful and he was all mine. I didn't even have a shirt for him to wear. How on earth was I going to do this? I knew deep down I was a survivor. Things would be okay.

After three days, it was time to go home. My mother surprised me by actually having a little sweater set for Dino to wear home. When we got to the house, there was nowhere for Dino to sleep. I took out one of the dresser's drawers, put a blanket inside, and that was his bed. Sofia and her family bought my son some t-shirts, pajamas, and bottles. Three weeks passed and someone gave us a bassinet for Dino to sleep in. Everyone was sweet to my son and I was very grateful for it all.

My mother received food stamps and welfare money for Dino and I. Yet I never saw a single penny of it. Back then, you couldn't have your own welfare case if you still lived with your parents so there was little I could do. I was forced to steal all of my son's formula, food, and diapers. I would even go into stores and steal clothes for him. Dino was growing and developing well but my concerns for him were heavy. I would cry myself to sleep at night. It was a horrible time for me. I never slept out of fear that someone would either fall on him or burn him with cigarettes.

After the second month, Dino could no longer sleep in the bassinet because he was too heavy. I began to panic. Out of desperation, I reached out to a guy I knew and told him about my situation. He said he would help me anyway he could with whatever I needed. I told him I needed a crib so he came by with one (as well as diapers and many other baby supplies). He clearly had feelings for me. Unfortunately, I didn't have them in return.

I never saw him again after that day. He called several times but I never picked up. I didn't want to use him or take advantage of his kindness. I needed to push through on my own and I did the best that I could when it came to loving, supporting, and keeping my baby safe. I never left Dino's side, not even for a minute.

~*
~

Being a mom becomes very disorienting for me. Although I can't quite understand the emotions, I can notice the shift in my actions. The Obsessive Compulsive behaviors have officially arrived. I'm determined to not fail my child. I made sure to hand wash all his clothes. I cleaned the house every day, all day. Everything was done ten times over to make sure it was perfect.

There was a woman named Ginny who lived down my mother's block who I had known for many years. Ginny was very aware of how dysfunctional my family was since she used to hang out from my mother and Annmarie from time to time. Ginny would always stop me to say hello when I walked around with Dino. One day, she took me by surprise when she said, "Donna, you take care of your son very well! You need to get him away from these people." I couldn't believe she recognized me. I was very moved by her words. I looked her in the eyes and simply told her, "I have nowhere else to go". I still remember her fondly.

Sometimes I'd go around the block while pushing Dino in his carriage to help him fall asleep faster. One summer night, while doing just that, I heard a very peculiar car honk behind me. It was one of those really loud and obnoxious song-like honks which were always hard to ignore. When I turned around, I didn't recognize the driver so I continued my walk. It didn't take long for me to realize he was honking at me. After a few attempts at starting up conversation, I finally said "hello" and he introduced himself as Tony. He pulls over to chit chat and we begin getting to know each other. We talked for about half an hour and parted ways after saying good night. I didn't expect to see him again.

Over the next few weeks it seems like Tony is always there (outside my house blowing that horn). He brings Dino food and takes me out to eat on occasion. We take Dino to the park together and continue getting to know each other on a more personal level. What a great guy. Always nice and always respectful. Tony treated my son and me very well and seemed to be there anytime I needed him. We'd visit his parents and siblings on a regular basis, which led to me becoming close to them (and at times even babysitting his nieces).

After dating for some time, I started wondering why we never hung out at his house. I asked him if we could go one day and to my surprise, he tells me he has three kids and lives with the mother. I couldn't believe what he was saying. I felt as though my life was over. He explained that he was only staying with her for the sake of the kids. Being that we spent every waking moment together, I believed him.

Although leery of what he tells me, Tony and I continue dating. Things are going very well. Tony and Dino have a special bond and I love the way they interact. It was always the three of us: Dino, Tony, and I. We were our own family. My mother would occasionally babysit Dino so Tony and I could go out to dinner and the movies. He was definitely a romantic. I loved taking walks on the beach with him and we were very sexually compatible. Perhaps that's why I shouldn't have been so shocked when I found out I was expecting a child.

~*~

I find out I'm pregnant at the emergency room. The doctor examines me, takes some blood work, asks me about medications as he orders a sonogram for me. When he comes back, the doctor explains to me that due to a medication I was taking the previous week for a kidney infection, the baby would probably not make it. If the baby did survive the pregnancy, it would be severely disabled. The baby would not develop corneas, would have Spinal Bifida, and a host of other disabilities. He insisted the baby would not be able to go home and would have to live in the hospital for constant care and supervision. He called it a "medically necessary termination". I was utterly devastated.

After seeing two other doctors for second opinions, Tony and I are faced with making the final decision on what to do with the baby. Afraid of having a miscarriage and feeling truly heartbroken, I realize I don't want my baby to suffer. Apart from the fact that continuing with the pregnancy could also hurt me, why would anyone knowingly bring an unhealthy child into the world? I set up the appointment for the termination as soon as possible. This was one of the hardest things I've ever had to do.

I arrived at the clinic with my mother. As I sat there, I realized many of the women that were waiting had been there before. They didn't seem disturbed or affected by what was about to happen. I could not stop sobbing. As soon as they called my name, I slowly walked in but the entire process seemed so fast. It was done. I no longer had a baby inside me. They gave me tea and a cracker right after. Apparently they won't let you go until you've had something to eat.

As soon as I get home, I go into the apartment and leave my mother in the cab. I can't stand to be with or around anyone. I'm devastated. The depression has set in. Tony comes home and tries to comfort me. He keeps telling me it's "going to be okay" and "we can try again" but at that moment, all I could think about is the baby that no longer was. I continue this way till I go back to my doctor three weeks later for a follow-up. The doctor tells me everything is fine and I immediately ask him, "When can I try again?" He tells me to give my body a few more weeks and try again. I was relieved to know that the possibility of having another baby was still real.

After a few months of trying with no results, the doctor sends me to a fertility clinic. I went to Mount Sinai in Manhattan. They took multiple tests of Tony and me to eventually find out that I had fibers growing in my fallopian tubes that stopped the sperm from meeting the eggs. I underwent a procedure to clean out the fibers and about after a week, I began trying again. They instructed me to have sex in the morning and by that afternoon, I got the call. I was two hours pregnant. It's incredible how even though I yearned to be pregnant again, now that it was real, I was scared. Dino was now four years old and I wanted him to have as sibling. Tony also wanted us to have a child together. He was the best thing in my life at the time and I figured everything would work out for the best. Little did I know how my life was about to change.

As I got further along in my pregnancy, Tony decided to get me an apartment. I thought it was great because that meant our relationship was moving forward. I never understood why the mother of his children lived with him. He was never there with her or his children but I figured my future with him was more important than his future with her.

At the new apartment, things were going nicely. My pregnancy was going smoothly. Dino was doing great and was happy to have his own room. Somewhere around the seventh month of my pregnancy, Tony pushes me into the wall. He starts to become very verbally and physically aggressive with me when he gets mad. I couldn't believe it. Who was this man? What happened to the man I had been with for the past three years? It got to the point where he was hitting me on a daily basis. The rages became more and more frequent every time. The weird thing is that Tony was very kind to me between his outbursts; he was the same loving man I fell in love with. When I was eight months pregnant, he kicked me between my legs as I was walking away from him. He continued to beat me right after that. By this point my entire world seemed to be crumbling around me.

As the abuse continues, Tony begins to hit me in public. It didn't matter where we were, whenever he was angry, Tony hit me. Many times people on the street would stop and say something to him but he never cared. It never stopped him. I always had a black eye and bruises. My mother started to notice. I always gave her excuses and brushed it off. She began to ask Dino about the bruises. Tony tried to hide the abuse from

Dino but it wasn't long before he no longer cared. By this point, I'm terrified for the baby inside me and how he's being affected by the abuse. I couldn't even stand up for myself. I was completely numb to the entire situation.

I did try to leave on multiple occasions while he was at work. I would pack my things and go to my mother's house. At this point, she knew Tony was hitting me. The only thing she would do is gossip to everyone about that fact that it was happening. Acting like a concerned mother was her specialty but in reality she just wanted the attention for herself. Tony would constantly show up trying to talk to me but my mother would always yell at him from the window. One day she even hit him in the face with a broom (which made matters worse). I knew in the back of my mind that I would be paying for that soon enough. Usually after about two weeks of being at my mother's, her constant degrading opinions about my life would lead me back at Tony's.

The abuse continued for the duration of the pregnancy.

Although the abuse was already an awful experience, having Dino stay at my mother's house and exposing him to what I experienced was much more upsetting to me. Even though Dino managed to witness the abuse often, he never asked or said much about it. I would always tell him that Tony was "in a bad mood". He was a calm and easy kid. My mother used to talk badly about me to him for some reason. I guess she always wanted to be *number one* in his eyes. He would later learn the truth about who his grandmother really was.

It's July and my water breaks while Dino and I are home alone. Dino laughed at me thinking I had "peed myself". I didn't want to call Tony. I didn't want him anywhere near me. I went to my mother's house instead and she and Annmarie took me to the hospital. As soon as I get there, the doctor examines me and tells me I'm crowning. He notices that the baby's head is blue. They decide to induce my labor. Not feeling much movement all morning, I start thinking the baby is dead. I immediately blame Tony's abuse. I'm dilating fairly fast and the baby's heart rate begins to speed up. The doctor tells me my baby is in fetal distress and they need to get him out as soon as possible. All of a sudden I go from lying on the operating table to being forced in an upright sitting position by the doctor. It was excruciatingly painful.

I don't know what is going on but there are many people in the operating room around me. As I look down, I notice my baby is half way out. The umbilical cord is wrapped around his neck three times and they're trying to cut it so he can breathe properly. His head was almost black at that point. The doctor cut the cord and the baby began to cry. As soon as I give the last push, my baby is out and immediately stops crying. The doctors and nurses rush to assist him and within minutes he is breathing, crying, and everyone starts clapping. I was so confused but so happy to know my baby was okay. I named him Nicholas.

My mother called Tony with the news and he showed up at the hospital. She couldn't stand him at this point and neither could the rest of my family so they all left as soon as he arrived. Tony immediately burst into his usual apologies: insisting he would do better and I foolishly always believed him. By now, did I really have a choice? I couldn't deny him seeing his own child. Yet I felt stuck in my life with two kids and nothing or no one else to support me but him. What the hell was I thinking? Maybe that was the problem; I wasn't thinking.

Nicholas was not doing well when he was first born. His head was still very purple and he began having tremors (his entire body would shake uncontrollably for brief instances). The doctors thought I had taken illicit drugs while pregnant although my blood tests showed otherwise. I refused to have them test my baby for drugs. They became very persistent but I still refused. My mother arrived with my pre-natal card (which showed when and where I took my prenatal care) which seemed to satisfy the doctors. Over the next three days, Nicholas' tremors become less frequent and his skin color becomes more normal. The doctor insists that he is doing much better and gives us the OK to go home.

~*~

Two weeks after being home with Nicky, the landlord tells me that we have to leave the apartment. She informs me that Tony hasn't paid the rent in a few months and she doesn't mind if I stay but he had to go. She knew he beat me and could no longer stand him living in the building. Unfortunately, I have no way to pay the rent on my own so the four of us end up moving out.

Tony finds an apartment on Apollo Street in Greenpoint. The landlords were a very sweet, older couple but our life there was crazy. I was always happiest when Tony didn't come home. I knew there were other women in his life by now and I had a much clearer idea of the real man he was. As much as he loved hitting me, Tony would always freak out when I threatened to leave his side

It was the 100th time I told him I was leaving after one of his violent outburst and my sister Bippy was visiting. Tony told me that if I left, Nicholas would stay with him. I knew I would never leave my kids so instead, I began looking for another form of escape. I decided I was going to try and jump out the window. We were on the first floor and I figured once I got out I would be able to call the cops. He kept beating me in the bedroom while the baby screamed and Bippy begged Tony to open the door. I somehow manage to convince Tony I wouldn't leave and just when he began letting me go, I made a run for it. I opened the window but as soon as my foot was on the ledge, I felt Tony right behind me. Out of fear, I immediately jumped.

Barely landing on my feet, I looked back to see Tony jumping out the window right behind me. I turned my face to avoid getting hit. His foot still landed right on it and his other foot landed on my knee. If that wasn't enough already, Bippy jumped on top of him causing me a lot of pain and pressure. I could feel the concrete scrape my face and I could feel things breaking inside my mouth. In my mind, I'm freaking out.

The poor, old landlords were sitting right at the stoop witnessing the entire sequence of events. I thought they were going to drop dead of a heart attack right then and there. Tony simply picked me up and carried my kicking-and-screaming-self back inside. I knew my mouth was fucked up at this point. What used to be teeth felt like loose tic-tacs in my mouth. I couldn't believe or understand my reality but I knew I still needed to find a way out. As soon as Tony sets me down I ran through the rooms and jumped out the window again.

I ran to my mother's house and called the cops. As soon as they arrived, the cops walked with me back to the apartment to get my baby. Tony tried to get smart with the cops by telling them to mind their business but they weren't buying any of it. For some reason, I still did not press charges against him. At this point, I was honestly more concerned about seeing a dentist. I knew if I pressed charges, Tony would take my son since he was "the breadwinner" of the two. I had to be smart. I had to think of my sons first and foremost.

My mother refused to take care of Nicky while I went to the dentist because she "ain't his father". After everything that had just happened, I was being forced to call Tony right back so he could pick up the baby. It always seemed to go from bad to worse. I couldn't escape the craziness. I honestly began thinking about ending it all but my children always changed my mind. They grounded me. I could never do that to them.

The very next day while at the dentist, I received the most devastating news. I had to have four teeth removed since they were shattered during the incident. There was no saving them. The dentist sat me down and removed every tiny, broken-up piece of tooth and bone. He then sewed my gums together. I couldn't believe it. I was twenty three years old and had no front teeth. On top of that, the very next day was Dino's Kindergarten graduation. I went home and cried for hours. What was I going to do? There was no way I could miss it.

The following day I spent the entire graduation with the flyer they handed out in front of my face. I was so embarrassed. But when my Dino sang his song, I was overjoyed just to be there. It was such a proud and happy moment for me. We celebrated with cake once we got back home. The very next day I was back at the dentist's office. He gave me a flipper device with four teeth on it to wear.

~*~

I still couldn't make sense of all the crazy shit in my life. It seemed to be one tragedy after another. My life had always been a windstorm of chaos and dysfunction. Now I had two kids of my own to add the complexity of it all. I'm not even sure how I was still standing or much less how I kept going. The landlord still needed us to move out but by now I started realizing I was at my mother's house every day anyway. I kept hoping she would stop opening the door to take me in only to talk shit about me like always. I was basically looking for a miracle. I stayed with her and her usual and constant bullshit for about a week. She drove me mad. I could not help but leave again.

With Dino and Nicky, and no place to go, I feel forced to go back to Tony. He decides to move us from Greenpoint, Brooklyn all the way to Ridgewood, Queens (in attempts at making it harder for me to run away). He knew exactly what he was doing. Once again, things went from bad to worse. We moved into an apartment on Bleecker Street but we weren't even there for a month. The landlord was very smart. She could tell exactly what type of person Tony was and she didn't like him. She was always kind to me though.

One night during one of his psychotic rages, Tony and I began to fight throughout the apartment. The landlord lived next door so she could hear everything. All of a sudden Tony picked me up by my throat and threw me across the room and onto the bedroom wall. I blacked out for a minute. The landlord started banging on the wall while screaming, "I'm calling the cops!" I opened my eyes and out of nowhere Tony has a butcher knife in his hand. He has it pressed against my throat. I can still feel it cutting into my skin. The landlord bangs again and Tony lets me go.

While Tony was at work the next day, the landlord knocked on my door to make sure I was okay. I tell her that I need to leave him and I can call some friends to help me move out. The landlord was nice enough to give me back the security deposit. She even offered me to stay with her and her husband in the meantime but I couldn't do that to them. When Tony got back from work that evening, the landlord didn't even let him in the building. She told him I no longer lived there and threatened to call the cops if he made a scene. Since we never put anything in writing, Tony knew he had no rights and left accordingly.

This time instead of going to my mother's house I end up heading to Peter's (since he was in Maspeth, Queens which was not too far from me at the time). I knew Tony would show up at my mother's looking for me so I wanted to avoid running into him at all costs. Peter was living with Sofia and their two children. They welcomed me and my sons with open arms. Dino and Nicky were very happy there and I adored spending time with my niece and nephew. It's sad to think that amidst all the abuse, the children were the only ones that truly brought me joy.

A couple weeks later, Nicky's grandmother calls me telling me she misses me and the kids and would like to see me. After making her promise that Tony will not be there, I decide to go visit her with Nicky. While having coffee and catching up, Angel (Tony's brother) stops by. At some point Angel gets a phone call from Tony. He tells him to come outside and they immediately start arguing over family finances. I motion to Angel not to tell Tony I'm there. I begged him not to go outside but he was a strong-willed man and went anyway. I think he figured that they would argue, maybe fight a bit, and that would be the end of it.

As Angel goes out the door he grabs a crowbar. He crosses the street and the arguing continues. From the window, I watch them while making sure Tony does not see me. After a few minutes of back and forth banter, the fight becomes physical. Fists are flying all over the place. All of a sudden, Tony reaches into his Cadillac and pulls out a gun. He aims the gun into the air and shoots. The bullet happened to be heading in my direction. Even though I saw the entire thing play out, I didn't think to move. It happened so fast that my brain didn't make the connection or the conclusion that it could potentially hurt me.

I stood still. The first bullet blew right through the window of the apartment above me. The second bullet rang out and Angel fell to the floor. Startled, Tony gets in his Cadillac and drives off. With Nicky still in my arms, I make sure Tony is really gone and rush downstairs to check on Angel. It wasn't long before I realized he was dead. I was crying over him when the cops pulled up. At first, the cops wanted to arrest me thinking I had something to do with it (probably since I was the only one by his side). I told the police who did it. They took me into the police station for my statement and eventually, Tony got arrested for his crime. To this day, Angel's dead eyes still haunt my dreams.

I was free of Tony's abuse which had kept me from living at my mother's house.

Even though I was free of him, my mind was so used to the chaos that the new-found freedom meant nothing to me. I had nowhere to go and I had no answers. And this time, I had to think of Dino and Nicky. One thing I've learned about domestic violence is that it doesn't go away just because the other person is gone. Years of abuse can destroy from the inside, leaving unresolved emotions that take and deserve time to heal. Although at the time I was staying at Peter's, Paul was going through a tough time and I felt being with him made more sense.

Paul was dating Sofia's sister, Patty for about four years and they already had two daughters together. By the time I came by, I realized Paul wanted me close because they were going through a separation. Although they both made mistakes, my main concern at the moment was my nieces and their well-being. I began living there to take care of the girls. Patty left and Paul was never really home. It was just me and the kids.

After about six months, Peter buys a house and agrees to let me live in the basement with all four kids as long as I pay rent. Things were falling into place. I felt like I was getting my life together for once. I began babysitting to make money. I enjoyed spending time with Sofia and her children, plus having all the kids around made it feel like a happy (and not purely dysfunctional) family. It felt like we finally had time to bond and grow as a family.

With Bippy and her girlfriend Lisa living right up the block, I never felt alone. They were always a major part of our lives. They loved my kids as though they were their own. Spending time with them, and making memories; my children loved them both very much. Bippy and Lisa would often buy my kids many things I couldn't afford. But what was most important to me was that they showed my sons love and affection.

Amidst all this, I decided to start a cleaning business and asked Sofia to be my partner. Babysitting was fine but it never seemed to bring me enough money. In the beginning, business was slow but eventually things picked up and we were making good money. We weren't rich but we made enough to live comfortably. Being able to buy "extra" things for the kids made me happy.

~*~

It was around this time I began noticing some odd behavior in Nicky and wondered if something was wrong. At first, I assumed it was just tantrums but as time went on his behavior became more and more alarming. There was a lot of screaming, yelling, and banging on walls. For some reason, Nick could not stay still for more than a few seconds at a time. I wasn't sure what to do to help. As his behavior became more and more disturbing to me, I began looking into seeking professional help to understand what could be causing it. I made appointments with a few different places for evaluation. I took him to a psychiatrist who was the first to diagnose Nicky with ADHD

(Attention Deficit Hyper-Activity Disorder) and ODD (Offensive Defiance Disorder). From there I decided to go for a second opinion so I took Nicky to Beth Israel hospital in Manhattan for a full eight hour evaluation. Beth Israel staff diagnosed him with the same disorders but also insisted he had Autistic tendencies (which I didn't see at all). At this point, I was devastated but I understood Nicky definitely needed professional help.

Nicky's behavior was so odd at time that it was as if he saw himself from a third person perspective. When asked if he knew what he was doing was wrong, Nicky would always acknowledge it was but never seemed to have full control over his actions. I decided to take him to a school for children with disabilities to be evaluated. They decided they could help him so he started going there once he turned three years old.

About a year passed but I saw very little change in his behavior. I finally decided to try medication since the doctors insisted Nicky had psychotic tendencies. I didn't like the idea of medication at all but at the time I felt like I had no other option. By now, I had read a variety of books on mental illness and Nicky seemed to fit every category. I was scared of the outcome but I had to do something to help so I agreed on having Nicky take medication for his ADHD. They started him with Ritalin. I thought his ADHD was bad beforehand but after taking it, Nicky seemed to have the ADHD of twenty one kids combined. The doctors kept telling me we had to be patient since the medication dose could only be raised slowly.

Nights were awful for the both of us. Nicky didn't sleep, therefore I didn't sleep. He just could never stop moving. He would scream all day and always get into mishaps that could easily hurt him (had I not been watching his every move so consistently). Nicky would climb up on the kitchen counter and run right through it barefoot. Right through the sink, the drain board, and all the glass dishes! His quick reflexes and ability to evade actual danger wouldn't leave room for him to fully consider the consequences. I always had to be very cautious and attentive. Life seemed incredibly overwhelming as a mother. I used to cry myself to sleep wondering how we would get through it all. Over time, the doctors prescribed many different medications since nothing seemed to help relieve his symptoms.

Things at Peter's were going pretty smoothly apart from all this. Finally having my own space to share with my kids and nieces made me feel more at peace. We made it into a nice home. I began understanding Nicky's behavioral shifts more and more but I was still unable to change any of it. Some of the behaviors would get better but usually as one would dissipate, another one would take its place. My world was spinning with thoughts and fears of failing my son. I knew I had to do anything I could to not let that happen. Soon after he aged out of preschool, Nicky was reevaluated. He started attending a public school through the special education program with the smallest class setting (seven to nine students). Even with a teacher and three paraprofessionals helping, Nicky was still a handful.

In the first grade, Nicky attempted to commit suicide for the first time. I got a call from his school telling me he was found hanging inside his classroom from the cord of the blinds. Nicky had hung himself. I'd never felt fear like I did when I heard what had happened. I told the school staff to wait until I got there before calling EMS. I rushed to the school to find Nicky sitting in the office as cool, calm, and collected as could be. He didn't even seem to understand what he had just done. I took him to St. Vincent's hospital in Manhattan. Little did I know it would be the first of many trips there. I was petrified. The hospital staff took us to the Child Psych unit and I gave them a brief description of Nicky and his behaviors. They spoke with him and decided to keep him overnight for observation. Even though I was scared, I was glad they had him overnight. I wondered if he would try to hurt himself again at home. I kept wondering what changed for him to make him want to do that in the first place.

I wasn't allowed to stay overnight with Nicky. It was so hard for me to leave him but I knew I had to do whatever it took to keep him safe. Dino was also having a hard time. He was scared for his brother and I was now fully aware this was a challenge that didn't just involve or affect me. I knew I had to educate myself on the various diagnostic labels, mental illness terminology, and specific characteristics. The weird thing was that Nicky seemed to have symptoms from all of them.

After thirty days of being hospitalized, Nicky returned home on a cocktail of medications but with minimal improvements. His ADHD was as active as could be and none of the medications seemed to calm him down. He slept about one single hour a night. I was mentally drained. I felt like Dino was not getting enough attention from me at this point. He was such an amazing and caring brother no matter what. Dino would always try his very best to deal with Nicky without getting angry. I would always try to spend one-one time with Dino so that he knew he was just as special and important to me.

Raising Nicky would prove to be the biggest challenge of my life but I was determined to succeed. His condition was frantic and exhausting but Nick was always happy child. His impulses were simply greater than him and lead to many of his antics becoming dangerous or alarming. Over the next few years, Nicky went through many more hospitalizations and medication trials. I feared taking him off medication would make things worse. I couldn't handle the thought of him trying to kill himself again. Even though life didn't seem to get much better, through it all I enjoyed both of my sons. I gave them all the love I could. Most of the time, we were happy. We struggled but we were happy and most importantly, we were a family.

~*~

Peter and I didn't always see eye to eye on things. It had been about four years since I moved into the basement and I didn't have many complaints. Until the day that Peter came down to my apartment and started arguing with me. He was upset because I took Sofia to get her eyebrows done; he was the jealous type. During the argument, he lifted his hand and smacked me in the head out of nowhere. That's when all hell broke loose. We got into a fist fight. I hit him in the head with a pot. He pulled out my hair. We fought and rolled around all over the kitchen floor. My kids were scared to death. It went on until he ran outside and called the cops (on me).

As soon as the cops arrived, they questioned us separately on what happened. By the time they got downstairs to me, the cops seemed to be under the illusion that my brother was doing me a favor. One cop stated, "Your brother allows you and your kids to live here!" I immediately replied, "Wait a minute! I pay rent! He isn't doing me any favors." Uncertain, the cops directed their attention to Dino and asked him if this was true. Dino told the truth. With a clearer understanding of what had occurred, the cops went outside and told Peter he could not enter my apartment without my permission. Much less should he put his hands on me. We both agreed to stay away from each other. I knew from that point on, it would never be the same between us.

Over the next few days, Peter and Sofia went out of their way to make me uncomfortable. Peter would tell me I could no longer sit on his stoop. I couldn't even spray my kids with his hose. Sofia simply avoided me. At this time in my life, I was still pretty violent (especially when it came to sensitive issues). The mere thought of my children's feelings being hurt by Peter's behavior would eventually trigger another physical altercation. For the sake of my sons I moved out and decided to do the unthinkable (again). Back to my mother's house we went (leaving Sofia with the cleaning business).

Before going to my mother's house, I put all my personal belongings and furniture in storage. I finally had my own belongings and frankly, I worked too hard to let them go. I strived to let my children know and love my mother as they should. Even though she and I would fight in front of them, I would always try to keep it to a minimum. Unfortunately the one thing I could never hide from them was her drinking. Still, she was their Nanny and I didn't want to deprive them of a relationship with her. Children deserve to know their loved ones.

Nicky's condition was serious and his environment was detrimental to helping him get better. I had him on a strict schedule with everything. This was crucial when it came to dealing with his disorder. Perhaps this is why I kept asking my mother and Annmarie to take it easy on the drinking and fighting. Nicky never seemed to be affected by their toxic behavior but I was aware that it wasn't good for him. By now, Dino is eleven years old. He was a sweet, caring boy who loved his grandmother to pieces. I never expected to see him burst out of my mother's room in tears one day.

When I asked him what was wrong, Dino tells me my mother has talked badly about me his entire life. She told him that I'm "a no-good mother" who "doesn't care about her kids". My mother even told him she was "the only one that truly cared about them". He couldn't stop crying as he told me all the things she had said. I looked Dino in the eyes and said, "Dino, now you know why I argue with your Nanny. She has always been this way; mean-spirited and vindictive." He clearly didn't understand but he kept telling me I *was* a good mom who loved and always took care of us. He begged me not to tell her what he told me. I never did because I knew he loved her.

I had to keep going. I started a new cleaning business with a friend for income. Things were going okay yet my mother and Annmarie's drinking was still out of control. My kids and I slept in a small bedroom that had a high-riser bed and a dresser. At night we would pull out the bottom bed for Nicky to sleep on. He constantly moved around in his sleep so I liked keeping him close to the floor. My mom had to walk through our room to get to hers. Always with a cigarette in her hand, she would drop her ashes on Nicky. I asked her not to smoke when she passed by but she would just say, "If you don't like it, get the fuck out!" I let it go and didn't say anything. I had no choice.

Two nights later, the kids and I are in bed when my mother comes through our room with a cigarette in her hand. As she passes Nicky, she stumbles and drops the cigarette right on his head. The lit part of the cigarette rolls down his head and into his ear. He woke up screaming his head off. I went nuts. I was so mad that I started yelling at my mother while she just went off on her same old "if you don't like it, get out" rant. But that day, I wasn't having it. I picked her up by the throat and threw her across the room and onto her bed. I got my kids dressed and packed us each a backpack of clothes. It was midnight and I was headed straight for the

Bronx to a shelter for families in need. I was done with my mother but I was scared shitless for my kids.

We arrived at the shelter around one thirty in the morning. As soon as my kids saw all the people outside the shelter, I could tell they were scared. I thought about turning back but I knew I had no place to go. Going back to my mother's house was not an option. Even though I couldn't believe I was there, I knew I had to do it for my children and their well-being.

That entire night we went through a lengthy intake process to see if we qualified as "homeless". The DHS (Department of Homeless Services) staff sent me to various rooms throughout the night. They asked me multiple questions about our health, past addresses, and even asked me if I had relatives in other states. I was later told that if I did, they were willing to pay for my travel expenses. I explained to them that my mother's house was unfit for children and I had no other family to go to. After answering all their questions, I waited on a bench to know where they were placing us. I didn't sleep at all that night but Nicky and Dino rested on my lap.

The next morning, DHS staff took us to a hotel in Elmhurst, Queens (an area I wasn't familiar with). They explain to me that we would be under investigation for the following ten days to determine eligibility. In the meantime, they would be going to each of my previous addresses to verify whether or not I could return to them. As soon as we arrive at the hotel, the manager checks us in. I felt very ashamed and defeated as a parent. I hated putting my kids through this entire ordeal.

We were assigned a room with bunk beds and a twin bed. It also had a table with two chairs, a mini-fridge, and a hot plate. The room smelled horrible; old cheese and dirty feet. We left our belongings and headed out to the nearest store for some essentials, as well as new bedding. As soon as we got back, I cleaned and disinfected the entire room till it was spotless. It wasn't home but it was ours for the moment. Once again, I didn't sleep at all. The kids woke up multiple times throughout the night. It was obvious they were disoriented but as soon as they'd see me, Dino and Nicky would relax and fall back asleep.

The next morning, the kids and I met with the hotel staff to sign some paperwork regarding our stay. We then went out to explore the area and find places to eat. We even found a local park where we ended up spending the rest of the day together. By the time we got back to the hotel it was already dark out. I kept this routine up for the next couple of days. It was the weekend and while I figured out their school situation, I wanted to make sure they spent the least amount of time in and around the hotel as possible.

I don't speak to anyone there. Yet as an observer I begin noticing the women around me. Many of them seemed to be selling their bodies. At night they stood outside in front of the hotel picking up men. During the day, some would even make their own children wait in the hallway while they were in the room with random men. It was beyond disturbing. The odd thing was that these women seemed to enjoy living this way. At the same time, others were noticeably on drugs. Sometimes they'd even be consuming them in front of the building. This life was not what I wanted for my kids.

All the shifts in the environment and the constant worry for my children began to weigh on me. A few years had already passed since my diagnosis of severe anxiety and agoraphobia. Yet I hadn't quite found the best way to cope. I felt as though I was functioning without much hassle until now. The entire situation at the hotel created more panic and fear which made my anxiety much worse. I wasn't sure how much more I could handle on my own.

After about nine days of staying at the hotel, I received a notice stating that I was ineligible. It stated that if I didn't agree with the decision, I had to go back to the Bronx and re-apply. Once I got there, DHS staff informed me that my mother told them I could still live with her. If the DHS discovers the applicant has suitable housing, he or she becomes automatically ineligible for services. I could not believe they were willing to send my children back to a home where someone hurt them. Making me go through the entire process again only to end up back at the same hotel was not what I expected at all.

Two more rounds of the exact same process only to get the same result: ineligible. This time we were sent to a hotel located on the Van Wyck Expressway. It had a strip club right next to it and a salt mine in the back. It was desolate. No stores. No markets. Nothing. This place was somehow even more chaotic than the last. Some women would sneak in men through the windows at night. Unfortunately, a couple of them were also stabbed and killed this way. This place was no joke. I called my mother to tell her that if she didn't tell the DHS the truth, I would have her arrested for burning Nicky.

As the investigation continues, we are even further away from the kids' schools. Most days I would drop the boys off, go to work, and finish in time to pick them up. My work partner would pick me up from Nicky's school and drop me off later. October was ending, work was slowing down, and it was getting colder outside. On the days I didn't have work scheduled, I would stand outside Nicky's school all day until he was let out. My agoraphobia was so intense at this point that I had no other option. It didn't feel much better once I received yet another ineligibility notice.

Back to the Bronx we go! It's been two months of this back and forth and we were exhausted. While at the Bronx unit I met with an advocate for people with disabled children. The advocate connected me with a lawyer who opened a lawsuit against New York City for the emotional distress experienced by Nicky during all these shifts. Nicky's episodes were continuous (with minor breaks in-between) and since he was already on so many different medications there wasn't anything else to give him. He needed stability. With the help of the lawyer's representation, I was able to get an exact date and time for when the investigation unit would be at my mother's.

I called Bippy to make sure my mother would answer the door for the investigation unit. As soon as they arrived, the investigation unit staff witnessed my mother so drunk that she fell off her chair. She began cursing and talking badly about me to them. They finally knew I wasn't lying and officially pronounced me eligible. Little did I know the process wasn't over. It was then explained to me that it could take up to two years to receive a Section 8 voucher.

Throughout our stay, Bippy and Lisa were the only ones that would come by the shelter to check up on us. They made sure I had enough money or food for the kids and would bring them small gifts which would always cheer them up. I was happy to see them each and every time. As soon as I told them we were finally found eligible, Bippy and Lisa were overjoyed for us.

~*
~

Now that we were in one set spot, I was able to change Dino's school and set up bus service for Nicky's school commute. I was frustrated at knowing we had to stay in a hotel but those were the cards I was dealt. I eventually had to stop working due to the fact I couldn't travel alone. Money was really tight. One thing I did have was excellent credit and lots of credit cards.

I went shopping. I bought a TV, video games, toys, bedding, clothes, pots, and pans. I learned how to cook on a hot plate. I tried to make it as nice as possible for the kids. Seeing that my sons had so much more than the rest of the kids who lived there, I started feeling bad. These kids would have to sit around in the halls while their mothers were off doing God knows what. I couldn't believe the scenarios I'd see from day to day.

Every time I went to the store, I would bring snacks (such as cookies or fruit) for the kids waiting in the halls. One by one they each became my little friend. I didn't really socialize with the parents but they didn't seem to mind their kids playing in my room with my sons. It was most likely a relief for them.

After a few months, I decided to seek help for my anxiety and depression. I wasn't doing well at all and I knew it was time to address it. I sat down with a therapist and began to tell her my story. She was shocked that I was still in one piece. The therapist said the damage I had experienced was so severe that she couldn't believe I was even in her office asking for help. Most people with similar experiences would be in jail or dead instead. It was that serious. To me, it was just another day.

My experience with different kinds of abuse and trauma as a child lead to my emotions becoming distorted. Yet as soon as I became a mother, I had to teach myself how to feel and how to express emotion properly. I guess I thought I had it all under control. Till I entered the shelter system... then I lost it. Overload hit me. Since it wasn't just about my life but it also involved and affected my kids, it took me for a spin.

Although I tried to downplay my emotions out of fear of losing my kids, my therapist saw right through it. She promised me that she wouldn't do anything to separate me from my children. She insisted she was aware I was a responsible mother and my kids were in no sort of danger by my side. She simply wanted to help me fix the damage that was so deeply a part of me. I actually gave her most of this book to read and she was heartbroken for me. She made me cry. I finally felt heard. She was an amazing woman and the help she offered me is something I will always cherish.

I started the medications but only took a quarter of what they instructed me to take. All my life I suffered from excessive everything. Excessive worrying, depression, stress, anxiety... anything else you could name. Yet I somehow managed. I was a very angry individual who used to fight all the time. I hated the world. I never slept. The medicine did seem to help. I was still myself but with less worrying, stress, anxiety and depression symptoms. The medication never changed me. It just helped me relax and cope with more ease.

During my time in the shelter, I made two friends. They encouraged me to begin going to church. I figured it would help the kids so I tagged along. Dino and Nicky enjoyed going to Sunday school and I enjoyed attending the service.

My whole life I felt like there wasn't a god. If there was one, he was clearly on vacation from my life. Later on, I began realizing that everything in life happens for a reason. Perhaps someday I'll know the reason for mine. At this time, I definitely believed there was some sort of Higher Power that helped me get through it all.

Only a few months after I officially became eligible, I received a call from my social worker. My Section 8 had gone through. I was so happy. Everything seemed great until I began looking for a place to live. The look on people's faces when I told them I had Section 8 amazed me. People would become very rude and look at me like I was the scum of the earth. I called every real estate broker I could and walked the streets for days looking for options. I passed by so many windows with signs that said "apartment for rent" and reached out. Still, nobody would help.

At some point, I received a call from a real estate agent who said I previously called him looking for help. He told me he had an apartment to show me. I checked my list of people I had contacted but his name was nowhere to be found. Still, I agreed to see the apartment because I knew I couldn't miss out on any chances. I did some research on the address and noticed the apartment was located in a nice neighborhood (Ridgewood, Queens).

As soon as I got there, I had a very pleasant interaction and meeting with the landlord. He was so nice and I was so excited that I basically walked in and said, "I'll take it!" The apartment wasn't fancy or big but it was going to be mine. After about three weeks, I was able to move in with the kids. The staff from the hotel even planned a house warming party for me. They all showed up at my new home and surprised me. It was at that moment that I realized some people in this world actually do care. Apparently, the staff had never done something like that for any of their past clients. I was so shocked! Life was getting better. My kids had their own home. It was just our little family and that made me happy.

~*~

When leaving the shelter system, I received a furniture voucher which I used to purchase essential items such as beds, dressers, and a dining table and chairs. They also supplied me with a box full of other essentials such as dishes, glasses, a broom, a mop, an iron, a toaster, a sewing kit... you get the picture. I was incredibly grateful for these things due to the fact that I had nothing. I lost all my belongings since I was unable to pay the storage fees.

I felt like we were on our way towards a normal life. The first thing on the agenda was changing the kids' schools. Then there was changing Nicky's medication (which always meant another hospital stay). His situation was too complicated for a quick outpatient turnover. Nicky was hospitalized for about three weeks and seemed to get somewhat better. I always felt as though the doctors were missing something. Yet they explained that it's very hard to accurately diagnose children before the age of ten. This especially rang true when the child in question fit various diagnostic categories. Still, I kept taking care of Nicky the best way I could.

During Nicky's hospitalization, the doctors once again recommended he be placed in residential living. I refused. They proceeded to call the ACS on me with the attempt to remove Nicky from my care. That didn't work. I was an amazing advocate for my son. By learning everything I could about mental illness, I wasn't the parent that stood before the doctors and allowed them to talk and do whatever they wanted without my full understanding. I knew my rights as a mother of a child with disabilities. Nicky's behavior was dangerous (to himself and to others at times) but I still felt like he had the right to a normal life with his family. I was not going to let them turn him into a test subject.

By now we had been out of the shelter for a year and a half. Nicky's emotional outbursts were out of control. It was time to really figure out what was wrong with Nicky. Even though I knew it would be incredibly stressful to be separated from my son for such a long time, I had to do it for my son. I felt stronger emotionally and physically at this point. I sat Nicky down and explained the process to him. He didn't like it and, of course, made a huge fuss. This was exactly the type of outburst the doctors at the hospital needed to see for themselves. Nick was admitted into inpatient care immediately. I was an emotional wreck. Even though I already knew this wouldn't be easy, it broke me down to leave him on his own for so long. I suppose I was used to caring for him myself, no matter what.

Over the next couple of months, I would arrive at the hospital as soon as visiting hours started and wouldn't leave until they ended. The trip from our apartment to the hospital took two and half hours (just one way) but I didn't care. I felt so bad for Dino since he had to endure the back and forth traveling but he didn't seem to mind. Dino loved his little brother.

While Nicky was in the hospital, I got to spend some quality time with Dino at home. When Nicky was home, life was mostly all about him. I was happy to finally be able to give Dino the attention he deserved. He was an amazing son and brother. I had never seen a child so understanding with his sibling. Nicky was also very loving towards Dino. As brothers, they always got along well. It was ultimately Nicky's inability to control his impulses that usually shifted my focus away from Dino. I always had to make sure Nicky was safe and wouldn't get hurt.

During this extensive hospital stay, the doctors diagnosed Nicky with Bipolar Disorder, ADHD, and ODD. After doing my own research, I realized that these diagnoses fit Nicky best based on his ongoing symptoms. Around the fifth month of his inpatient stay, the doctor started Nicky on new medication. Things finally began turning around. It was a miracle: all of a sudden the aggression was gone. Nicky wasn't perfect, but I was glad to see him getting better.

I decided it was time to find a bigger apartment since the room Dino and Nicky shared was so small. I came across an apartment with three bedrooms and knew it would make life much easier for us. By this time, Dino was a teenager and Nicky wasn't too far behind. We all needed our own rooms. Nicky had a short attention span so I figured having his own space would be good for him. I overloaded his room with toys to keep him occupied and active once he came home from the hospital.

I began making many new friends and they soon became just like family. All the kids felt like my own. Especially one little girl named Joshalynn, who stole my heart. She was such a sweet child and she loved me very much. Spending time with her was always so fun. Some would say she is like the daughter I never had (and I would agree). As a little girl, Joshalynn was always happy and never complained. I would take her to the zoo and to the park as much as I could. She was a truly blessing in disguise.

When we first moved in, I began taking Nicky home on weekend passes. I never quite realized just how much work Nicky was until he went away and came back. Don't get me wrong, I was well aware he was a handful but it had already been a few months without him. I had to get used to it all over again. At least I got a break for a few months while knowing he was in safe hands at the hospital. Or at least, that's what I thought.

I received a call from Nicky crying while telling me a staff member hit him. I went bananas. I got to the hospital faster than ever. I almost got arrested when I got there since it was after visiting hours and I kept demanding to see him. With the cops present, staff eventually allowed me to see Nicky. I couldn't do much at the time but I assured them I would be back first thing in the morning to pick him up.

When I arrived to the hospital the next morning, I noticed a scratch on Nicky's neck. I called the cops immediately. When questioned, the staff member claimed it was an accident. He said it happened when he tried to restrain Nicky. What they didn't know was that Nicky had taken off the shirt he was wearing during the incident and hid it behind his dresser drawer. He brought out the ripped shirt to show the cops and I knew my son wasn't lying. Right then and there, I demanded that Nicky leave with me. Both the cops and I knew staff had attempted to disguise what had happened.

The staff called the ACS telling them I was trying to remove Nicky from the hospital prematurely. I had to leave but I couldn't take Nicky with me. The very next morning, I met with ACS and the doctors. Once I told ACS what had happened to Nicky they began to question the doctors intensively on Nicky's condition. As soon as they found out Nicky was doing much better on his new medication, ACS realized there was no reason for him to stay in the hospital any longer. Nicky was released to me.

When we got home, Nicky was ecstatic. He was so excited to see his new room. Life began feeling normal again. Nicky's outbreaks and mood swings were still present but not as frequent as before. I enrolled him in school and his therapy set up and scheduled. We were back on track. My family was still together and we were happy for the most part. I was still dealing with so much of my own at the time. I was slowly learning how to be a human being. I had to teach myself everything I could to be a productive parent to my kids.

Dino was growing up nicely. He had many friends and graduated from junior high school. Nicky was also doing well and was incredibly smart when it came to school. School work itself was never an issue for him. It was other things such as social interaction and making friends that were difficult for him in the long-term.

Even after everything that happened (and against my therapist's advice), I continued to visit my mother who now lived in Ridgewood as well. I helped take care of all of her needs and even painted her house when she needed help. I used to tell her, "as long as I can see you as a person, I will treat you well. But don't ever give me advice on parenting my kids".

By now my mother couldn't do a single thing to faze me. I was taking good care of my sons without anyone else's help. This was something she could never do herself. I think my success as a parent reminded her just how much of a failure she was. I took my mother to family therapy but as soon as she was presented with certain questions she ignored the situation. Pretty much any question that would make her own up to her actions would make her mad and cause her to walk out. My mother seemed to live in this fantasy world where she was a great parent with seven kids she raised wonderfully.

In reality, my mother destroyed us mentally and emotionally for the sake of her own selfish needs. Even at this point, my mother would call me out of the blue and drunk off her ass talking shit. I would simply tell her to go fuck herself. She would then call everyone crying and telling them I had treated her like shit. Always playing the victim. Once in a while, my mother would say things like, "I wish I was like you". Only to follow it up with a statement such as, "you're a horrible mother". It was unbelievable but it was just the type of person she was.

~*~

Making long-lasting friendships with people around me was something I was unable to do well in the past. I had no tolerance for other people's bullshit but over time I learned to accept people for who they truly are (as well as find ways to appreciate them). I was always good at helping others. It seemed to make me feel good about myself. Maybe in my mind I was really just helping myself. Who knows? I still enjoyed doing it. To this day, I'm still the same way. Except in the past, I used to lose sleep thinking about other people's problems. Most of those people didn't even give a fuck about me. It's funny how people always seem to want something when you're offering it as a giving person. Yet the minute you say no, all of a sudden you're the bad guy. People seem to take advantage of another person's kindness. I wish I had a friend like me when I was growing up.

For the first time in my life I was feeling good about myself. I was still struggling with my inner demons and my social skills were horrible. I didn't even know how to joke around with others since I took everything so seriously. I never allowed the world to see that side of me. I guess I learned something from my mother after all. She hid the truth and I hid the pain. I used to believe that if the world saw your pain, it made you weak. I've been that way for as longs as I can remember. It wasn't till I got older that I realized the best thing I could do for myself was learn to grow and become a better person for the sake of my children.

Since the day I first gave birth, my goal was to get better each day for myself and for my children.

I was still in therapy. My therapist was great and she helped me understand all of my emotions and why I felt them. For years I assumed I was crazy but in reality, I was quite sane. I knew that what was going on in my life wasn't normal. Since I didn't know what normal was I had no way to change it. Finally someone confirmed what I already knew. She helped me differentiate between a normal life and the abnormal experiences I lived through.

I threw myself into my sons' lives in order to make every moment count. Although I was suffering from severe PTSD, depression and anxiety, for the first time in my life I was in control of my emotions. I was a product of my environment. Sometime that can be worse than having a mental illness. A lifelong habit is incredibly hard to break. Every aspect of my life was altered from such a young age due to the way I was raised.

I knew I couldn't change the past but I could change my future. First thing on the list was to get rid of my aggression. I now realized that the entire world was not my enemy and didn't know anything about me or my story. The most important part about changing your life is changing your environment. I no longer lived in the neighborhood where my mind was haunted the most by bad memories. That was a big part of my healing process. I no longer felt the need to hit someone or something just because I was mad. I said goodbye to my aggression from then on.

Next on my list was empathy. I wanted to learn how to empathize with others. I had to learn that there are no differences in any of our lives whether good or bad. I learned that people were allowed to get angry without me thinking "you're an asshole".

One by one, I learned to experience normal emotions. The hardest one was happiness. It's funny because even to this day being happy is still difficult for me. I often think the worst. I guess old habits die hard. Even if the pessimism never fully goes away, at least I'm not blowing up every time something goes wrong. We only have one life and if we don't strive to change it ourselves, it will never happen on its own.

Dino's high school graduation was such a proud moment for me. Not only had he finished all his schooling on good terms but he wanted to continue his education and head to college. I was ecstatic! This was wonderful news for a mom to hear from her son. I decided we had to celebrate and threw him a huge party! I had made it through his "teenage bullshit", which actually wasn't bad at all. He was all grown-up and I couldn't be more proud.

Nicky was also doing very well throughout his schooling, despite the fact he had many breaks due to his mental health.

Thankfully most of the hospitals were Nicky stayed as a youth provided him with classes and resources to continue learning. I decided to transfer him to a community high school to see how it went and if he liked it. At first Nicky did well. He tried so hard but eventually the transition was just too much for him. It broke my heart to see him struggle. After a year of public school, I decided to sign him out.

Around this time, Nicky decided to discontinue his medication. I believed Nicky had the right to make his own decision being that he was eighteen at the time. Still being aware he needed to be on medication, I went ahead let him taper off. He wanted to live life without meds and I respected my son's decision (even though I didn't fully agree) since I knew all too well how it feels to not fit in with others.

I love my sons more than life itself. My two boys are the reason I'm standing here today. Without them, I don't know where my life would be. They are and will always be my reason to live. I adore every aspect of being a mother; the good and the bad. I took parenting very seriously; always insisting I would never do to my children what my mother did to me. I know I didn't get everything right but my best intentions were always present. Ultimately, I believe there is no such thing as a perfect parent.

As a little girl, Joshalynn became and still is the apple of my eye. I thank her mom for allowing her to spend so much time with me. We have a connection most people wouldn't understand. Her mom is still a very close friend of mine. We are like family. We are together all the time. Joshalynn has grown to be an incredible young lady. She has graduated high school and is on her way to college. I couldn't be more proud.

I have made bonds with people that will last a lifetime. Never did I imagine that would be something that could happen. Life is a struggle all the way. People are all different. We choose who we remain close to by how much we accept from one another. I learned it is possible to be friends with people who are different than me. Deep down, we are all the same just with different qualities. There are people that you will meet and simply not like. And that's okay. You don't have to like everybody. And everybody doesn't have to like you. You won't always find people that think the same way as you. That's okay too. I learned how to treat people as equals. My life's journey was about me and no one else.

I only speak with my two brothers: Paul and Bob. I love both of them very much. Paul is still struggling with drug use but I'm always praying for the best. My nieces have grown up beautifully; such loving and caring girls. I hold them very close to my heart. Bob is doing well with his wife and their three sons. Although I don't see them as often as I'd like, I love my nephews very much. Even though I no longer speak to Peter or Sofia, I miss my niece and nephew dearly.

One person I truly adore is my sister Bippy. We've been together from day one and I couldn't be more proud of her. Both Bippy and Lisa have always been there for me and my kids. I have eternal gratitude to the both of them for always thinking of us. They are both terrific people through and through. I truly couldn't have asked for a better person as my sister. I'm at peace knowing that if and when something happens to me, Lisa will be there for Bippy no matter what. Lisa and Bippy gave me the best gift a sister could get: a beautiful niece and goddaughter named Skyla-Rose. We love each other very much. She is my sunshine forever and ever.

Our little family of three is doing well. I'm still trying and doing my best for my sons. Both Dino and Nicky are living productive lives. Dino graduated college and landed a great job. I am proud of the genuinely humble and hardworking man that stands before me each day. Nicky has also worked hard amidst all the hardships and obstacles and is constantly finding new ways to get to where he wants. I am very proud of Nicky and love him just as much. For now I will continue to help and do what I can for the boys and for myself. That is all I can do in life. Work hard and enjoy it as much as I can.

Sometimes I still feel broken inside. However, I have accepted that it's ok to be broken. There isn't always a spectacular ending of riches and fame. At times, all that is left is you and the fact that you survived all the things life has thrown your way. I don't strive to be perfect anymore. I am as perfect as I am ever going to be. The hardships, the terror, and the abuse come and go; sometimes just being okay is the best result you can get. I'm living my life without fear or worry.

As for anyone who is reading this: I hope my story has inspired some small aspect of your life. Maybe in some way my ability and need to share these experiences and thoughts can help you continue to go forward and onward. Or at the very least help you not give up. The rewards of our effort always come back to us in one form or another.

Made in USA - Kendallville, IN
16461_9798596969634
12.02.2021 1806